Christopher Lowell's
You can do it!

small
spaces

Christopher Lowell's
You can do it!

small spaces

Decorating to Make Every Inch Count

Clarkson Potter/Publishers
New York

Copyright © 2003 by Christopher Lowell
Photographs copyright © 2003 by Douglas Hill

Published by Clarkson Potter/Publishers, New York, New York
Member of the Crown Publishing Group, a division of Random House, Inc.
www.randomhouse.com

CLARKSON N. POTTER is a trademark and POTTER and colophon
are registered trademarks of Random House, Inc.

Printed in Japan
Design by Maggie Hinders

Library of Congress Cataloging-in-Publication Data
Lowell, Christopher.
Christopher Lowell's you can do it! small spaces :
    decorating to make every inch count.—1st ed.
    Includes index.
    1. Small rooms—Decoration—United States. 1. Title: You can do it! small spaces II. Title
NK2117.S59 L68 2003
747'.1—dc21   2002192656

ISBN 1-4000-4727-7
10 9 8 7 6 5 4 3 2 1
First Edition

This book is dedicated to my sister Laura. Because we moved so much as children, her friendship always gave me a feeling of "home." Her courage and unconditional love have kept our scattered family in touch. Her level head and honesty have kept me grounded in sometimes heady experiences. We always dreamed of working with each other. That dream came true when she joined my staff full-time last year as head of our information line. She commu-

nicates to hundreds of our viewers each and every day in efforts to keep her brother's "self-esteem ministry" and our loyal fans at the epicenter of everything we do. After years of struggle, she finally moved into her very own brand-new home. Like many of you, she now faces the challenge of infusing her new small spaces with all her passion and nurturing spirit. If her home truly becomes an accurate reflection of who I know her to be, and who I know she dreams of being, it will be a place like no other. It will be a creative mecca that, once again, I, too, can call home!

TOP: Me, age nine, and Laura, age five, with Mom's Mini and Mickey Mouse Birthday Cakes. We were born the same day and the same hour four years apart. Who knew? ABOVE: Laura. LEFT: Thirty-seven years later at an Emmy award ceremony. We are as close today as ever. Love that, love her!

contents

foreword

ORE THAN ANY OTHER SHOW THEME we do each year, small spaces seems to be the topic everyone can relate to. With the ever-escalating price of real estate, many who thought they would upgrade to larger homes found the cost prohibitive. For others, the relatively minor difference in value, dollar for dollar, simply didn't justify the move. Instead, folks across America are tearing down walls and reconfiguring their existing spaces to reflect a more open, modern, technology-compatible environment. Many are simply working with the small spaces they have only to find themselves stuck in the box. And for a variety of reasons small spaces seem to confound those not used to thinking outside the box.

So how do you get from single-function, cramped one-dimensional to multi-functional style in an 8-by-10-foot room? Well, my team and I stepped up to the plate to consider one of the most ambitious challenges we had ever faced and, frankly, hit one out of the park!

It began with an offer from Fleetwood Homes, a company that makes prefabricated houses in their factory then ships them to installation sites all over the United States. The team was shown to an open field where two homes sat side by side, still on the wheels that would transport them to Arizona four months later. We began our walk-through in 110-degree summer heat (not exactly conducive to creativity) taking Polaroids of every inch of these homes. With sweat dripping down onto our sketchpads, we began the process of designing each house room by room. When complete, one would be modern with a Zen attitude, while the other (of a similar floor plan) would appear more traditional, but with an updated contemporary twist. Some of the rooms were so small we had to back our cameras into the closets just to record our progress. These architecturally challenged spaces with their off-center fireplaces, underscaled windows, absent entry halls—and vaulted ceilings to boot!—storageless bathrooms, and dining rooms minuscule or nonexistent had us all scratching our heads.

But think about it: These structures are a remarkable value for those who couldn't otherwise afford to either own their own home or enjoy the luxury of a second vacation home. In fact, many of Fleetwood's houses, which range in size from approximately 640 feet to more than 2,300 square feet, start at $19,500. Even with that in

we still wondered if they could actually be transformed into the kind of

places we're known for. But that challenge only excited us more

ever. Never say never to the Christopher Lowell team.

ithin weeks we started solving the key problems. And by the end of

nonth we knew these modest houses would help us create one of our

seasons ever on *The Christopher Lowell Show.*

he following pages give proof that with imagination and careful plan-

even the most challenging spaces can be transformed from the ordinary

the absolutely extraordinary. Not only were we excited about dealing

the very real issues our viewers tell us they face every day in their own

es, but the opportunity to document our own creative process from begin-

; to end seemed even more valuable. Our publishing partners at Clarkson

er confirmed our enthusiasm when they immediately green-lighted the proj-

without hesitation.

f you are familiar with my step-by-step Seven Layers of Design approach (see

e 166), then you will probably recognize that *You Can Do It! Small Spaces*

es the fundamentals one step further. In these pages you will be able to watch

and my design team think out loud and think outside the box.

If we seem proud of this book, we are! If the makeovers seem too good to be

e, they're not! If you think you can't do it, YOU CAN!

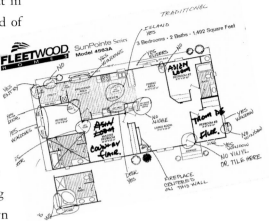

ABOVE: Floor plan of what became known to the team as the Traditional house.
BELOW: Our two Fleetwood Homes where they began life in Riverside, California. The Modern house is in the foreground, and the Traditional is in back . . . or is it the other way around?

introduction

WISH I COULD SHOW YOU the thousands of letters we receive about people who are tearing their hair out trying to find more living space in their homes. Some of them are obviously directly related to lack of square footage, but many dilemmas could be easily handled simply by getting rid of the clutter. Clutter is the number one handicap of most rooms. Evidence of that is the boom in storage containers, which manufacturers and retailers can't keep in stock, even in my own home collection. I'm all for decorative storage, but by making containers attractive, it gives us an excuse to hold on to everything we have ever owned, whether we need it or not. And now that we can stash our stuff in handsome receptacles that can be placed on tippity-top open shelving (where we'll NEVER see what's inside again, EVER) we think we have handled the clutter issue. In fact, all we have really done is procrastinated one more time about pitching the clutter.

POVERTY CONSCIOUSNESS

Why? It's because we are innately pack rats. We're told from childhood to "waste not, want not." My family was a family of savers. My Sicilian grandmother tore paper napkins in half and even found a way to recycle eggshells and coffee grounds. She would go to the produce section and hoard as many plastic produce bags and twisties as she could get away with. Even my other grandmother, who was somewhat more well-to-do, would dine at an expensive restaurant and then squirrel away all the sweetener packs and extra dinner rolls that her Nantucket basket would hold. One time, several of the packets were open and I, embarrassed beyond belief, had to escort her out of the restaurant leaving behind us a trail of Sweet 'n Low. How many times did I hear my own mother say, "There are people who have nothing," or "Children in Africa are starving, so stop your whining"?

But, while I feel that one should be a good steward of one's money and that cavalier spending should be frowned on, there is a limit. A lot of why we hold on to things we don't like or don't need is that the poverty consciousness we grew up with comes back to haunt us. There used to be time to "tinker in the garage," to repair those things that might be irreplaceable. But who's got that kind of time today? And are manufacturers really making things in such a way that even experts can repair them? Is it realistic to let a now-useless object take up valuable space when you know that in spite of your good intentions, the object in question will never get fixed?

I JUST HAD TO HAVE IT!

The flip side of the desire never to let go is the impulse to buy something we really don't need in the first place. What about one of those "seal-a-meal" or "salad shooter" gadgets that you simply had to order off that late-night infomercial? What about that enormous freestanding cooking machine that places poultry in the chamber of torture? Then you find out that it takes longer to clean than your entire oven. Yet, you tell me your kitchen is too small. We can't help it. We say to ourselves, "It's perfectly good. I can't toss something perfectly good, can I?" No, but you could give it to someone who could really use it.

Think of it this way: If we are how we live then what does your clutter say about you?

The reality is that we fill our lives and our homes with things we thought we needed and don't leave room for things we think we can't have. In other words, made room for the only life we thought we'd get but never left space for the life we might be able to have. I can't think of anything sadder.

A cluttered physical interior is a sign of a cluttered mental interior. It keeps us from dreaming about who we want to or could be. It's simply proof of what we were. Look around you. Does your home make room for the new or the old you? Is there space to evolve—to dream? Or is it a graveyard of things that remind you that your home really doesn't nurture you as it should? If your home is a place that doesn't allow for change, there's a reason for that.

CH·CH·CH·CHANGE!

In our hearts, we want everything to be new, fresh, and different, but in our minds, we don't want anything to change. Hmmm. Funny, but in nature birds build their nests one piece at a time. For months they toil around the clock. But after their chicks clear out of the nest, they abandon it. They're off building the next one not knowing what nature or fate has in store for them. They instinctively fall into a rhythm of life, unafraid. But we who have dominion over them and an opportunity to *make* choice, fear that choice most of all. Only after it is threatened to be taken away from us, do we wake up.

It's unfortunate, but a disaster like September 11 made a lot of us look around at our homes and say, "Gee, this place I call home may be the only thing I get that I have control over." Still, we place the blame for our lack of attention on our homes on—our homes! "It's too small, it's too expensive to fix, and it's so not me!" As though the house is in control and not us. As though our clutter rules instead of us.

In smaller homes this comes up more frequently. We seem to live with the idea that when we can afford it we will upgrade to more roomy surroundings, but for many of us, for many reasons, either we can't move right now or we never will. *Can't* is a word that causes resentment, so we grow unhappy with the home we are living in now. We hate what we have because it is a reminder of what we think we can't have. We live resigned to things staying the same or put our lives on hold until we think that we can upgrade. Somewhere in the future we'll take responsibility for that *new* home—that new life—that place altogether different from this one. For now we'll suspend any form of nurturing. Why spend all that time on a home that either isn't worth fixing up or is simply temporary?

I have heard this refrain all too often. I have also received many photos from viewers who paid heed to what we teach every day. After accepting where they really were in time, they did remarkable things with what they had—with astonishing results. From pitching clutter to tearing down walls, to turning occasional guest rooms into more useful creative spaces, they told us they had given themselves a new lease on life.

Everyone had a different story, but a number of our older viewers who had kept their empty nests the same after the kids moved out felt too guilty to make changes. They reasoned that if they converted their kids' old rooms into adult rooms, then the kids might not come back—or, if they did, then where would they stay? It finally dawned on these older viewers that if and when their "kids" did come back, they would be adults, not kids anymore. When they realized that they were hanging on to the past and hoping life would return there, they got the message. Retirees turned bedrooms into offices and actually started new businesses in their homes. If that's not life-changing, I don't know what is.

YOUR STUFF WON'T SAVE YOU

Our homes are not there to preserve what we *were;* instead, they should become incubators for who we want to *be.* Imagination, forethought, cleverness, and physical labor cost nothing. And frankly, small spaces are no less of a challenge than large spaces, because the same questions still pop up: "Who am I?" "What's

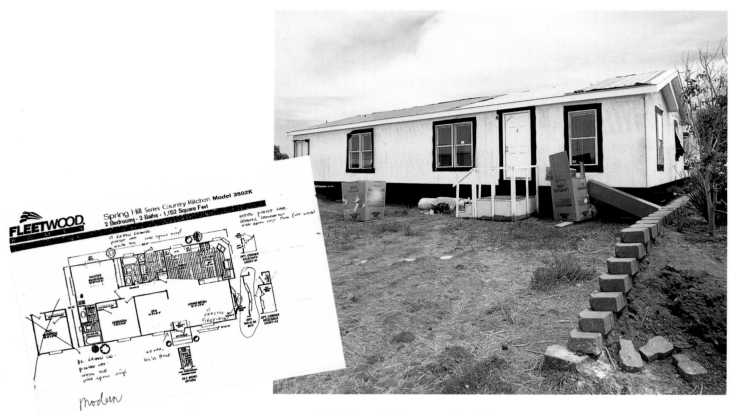

ABOVE: Floor plan of what my team called the Modern house.

my style?" "How do I want to live?" "What am I going to have to do to make this place a positive reflection of myself?" All that changes is the scale. The rest, my dears, stays the same, except for large spaces you need more stuff. You have to make more decisions and . . . well, you get the idea. So it should not be the house's fault that you can't find it within yourself to take a fresh look around you and be grateful for the chance to make change in one of the most profound ways you ever will.

THERE ARE NO SMALL SPACES, ONLY SMALL MINDS

Small spaces are only small in your mind, but still are a wonderful canvas on which to explore your universe. And we should explore that universe unabashedly with sentiment, naïvete, and wonder. Embrace what you find. Honor that with which you can connect. Whatever you no longer have feeling for, make it go away. Either pitch it or disguise it and make it into something else . . . but do something! When you do, then share it with those you love. Your home should inspire you. It should keep your creativity kindled and allow you to express your joy at the chance you have been given to claim your space and make it yours.

ENROLL, ENROLL

Remember, rarely does anything magnificent happen by itself, so once you have got an idea that you feel you have the courage to start and finish, then enroll. Enrolling others in your dream is about inspiring them with your vision.

Look at every inch of your home and ask yourself, "Is that space there, where the file cabinet is, the one I haven't opened in two years, better used for something else? Are those cupboards full of stuff I keep rummaging through to find the three things I actually do use ready to go bye-bye? Are those boxes, which fill my garage, full of things that only validate who I *was?* Or would this garage be better as a great living space for me to explore who I want to become?"

As you begin to look at how you have been living, write down what it is in your home that doesn't work. Make a note of what's missing that would make your space great. Windows can be added (real or otherwise); walls can be rearranged or painted; furniture can be covered or reupholstered; cubbies, book-shelves, and ledges can be added to help reorganize. Do what I do. Take the drawers full of stuff you've forgotten about and put them up on your bed. Turn on the TV or rent a stack of great movies. Sit there with a garbage bag while you watch a great film and start the weeding process. Don't stop there. Pile all your clothes on your bed and start going through them, too. If you haven't worn something in two years, you won't ever again. Give it away. Be ruthless, knowing someone will love what you are about to part with.

NOW, VOYAGER

Pretend you are moving onto a boat, a wonderful yacht that will take you all over the world. The price to pay for the adventure is to take only what you really need. It is said that he who travels lightest, travels farthest. Get rid of the extra luggage. Don't spend the rest of your life at baggage claim waiting for the stuff that has lost meaning for you to come off the conveyor belt. Give yourself a few weekends to accomplish this. Once you get started, I promise you won't be able to stop. It's addictive. Giving yourself a new life is exhilarating. At this stage it won't cost you anything but time. But not doing it could cost you everything!

RENTERS

I hear this excuse all the time: "I can't do anything because I live in an apartment." In my many years of living in apartments, I simply went ahead and did whatever I wanted to, and told the landlord nothing. Of course, I had to pay a price to return the place to the way I found it. But my improvements were usually better than the original and I rarely had a problem finding someone who wanted the apartment just the way it was. Be that as it may, even if you only paint and put up pictures, knowing you might have to slap on a few coats of white when you move, isn't it worth spending a few hundred dollars to give yourself the feeling that you have claimed your space and made it yours? If you divide the time you'll be there by the money it will take to make the place a reflection of who you are, you'll be surprised that the math comes out to pennies a day. Excuse me, but isn't your self-esteem worth it?

BOMB SHELTERING

Learn not to hoard. When you're out shopping at a flea market or if someone wants to give something to you, politely step back. Ask yourself, "Do I need this? Just because it's free or cheap, will I love this when I get it home, or does this simply get tossed on my home junk pile?" I know it's hard to resist, especially if the object is free, or if your son or daughter is hanging on your arm begging for a toy, but you owe it to yourself to summon restraint.

Believe me, I do this, too. But here's my rule. I say to myself, "I have everything I want. If I find something better than what I have, then I MUST replace it and give what I had to someone else." That means I can't keep both. Be realistic about your time. A perfectly lovely dresser that could be stripped, refinished, and newly adorned may be worth the $30 you might pay for it. But will you really *do* the work, or will it sit in the garage with everything else you said you'd redo. Will it be yet another reminder that you haven't followed through? Just because you *can* doesn't mean you *will.*

All in all, we need to find ways to fall in love with the potential of how our homes and our lives could be. It's so vital that we live in the moment instead of the past or the future. If you can discover something that will give you the nurturing you need today, then have faith that when you get to the next juncture in the road, you'll have the clarity to do it even better. Life is not a dress rehearsal; it's opening night, every night. So don't let anyone but *you* write your script or design your set.

INSPIRATIONAL ICONING

In my second book, *Christopher Lowell's If You Can Dream It, You Can Do It!*, I invited you to take the abstract ideas that rattle around in your heads and use them as creative launching points—springboards, if you will—to getting started in the design process. If certain objects in your home have ceased to have meaning for you, then they are just clutter, room dandruff that you accommodate rather than icons that inspire you. Consider giving these things to someone who can really use them and will have a connection to what, for you, is now simply meaningless "stuff."

Meanwhile, focus on what matters. Any object can spur creativity. A piece of china, a decorative pillow, even an article of clothing can have subtle meaning. In my case, in the makeover that follows, I was searching for a way to find a simple element to unify a very undefined living room/kitchen/den space.

Some ten years ago, I bought a model sailboat. It represented my love for the sea and the years my family lived aboard our boat—all that coastal living means to me. However, one day I began to study its hull construction. Two colors of wood were interrupted by dark horizontal lines.

I got my staff focused on it. And before long we had come up with a way to translate this element into the room. As a matter of fact, it really ended up becoming an integral component to the room's overall design. All that from a few lines on a boat model. Who knew? The truth is you never know how a simple visual clue or feeling can help connect you to how you may want to live. So try it!

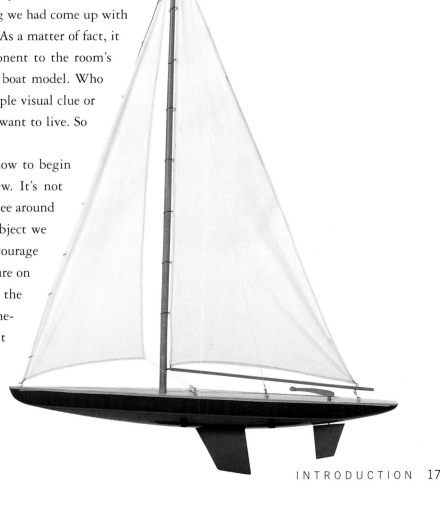

Throughout this book we will show you how to begin the design process from many points of view. It's not magic—it's just learning not to take what we see around us for granted. Remember, every man-made object we see is a result of someone's idea and his or her courage to bring it into the third dimension. The texture on a sponge, the clasp on a handbag, and even the color of a hybrid daylily was designed by someone or something. Visual clues can be right under our noses, and a trained eye and a fearless heart can take these icons and turn them into new objects of desire.

You can do it, too!

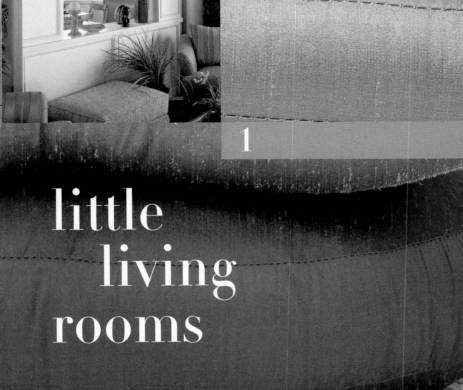

1

little living rooms

modern
living room

IT'S AMAZING HOW AN ICON can inspire a flood of creative ideas. But how do we take feelings from icons and translate them into three-dimensional form?

The inspiration for this living room began with that model of a wooden sailboat I mentioned in the Introduction. What I was attracted to was not the ship itself, but the horizontal line that looked like a wood inlay along the ship's hull. In the room horizontal lines already appeared on the fireplace mantel and the shelves of a room divider on the opposite wall between the living room and kitchen. We could have ignored these elements and introduced strong vertical archi-

tecture to the room, but instead, remembering the icon, we looked for ways to continue these horizontal lines all the way around the room to unify the space, transitioning the lines into everything from seating to merchandising ledges to storage shelves. As we progressed through the room's Seven Layers, we added vertical gestures in the form of accessories, lighting, and plants.

The only feature of the wall area at the end of the room was a triple bay window in the center. The decision was made to build a modular shelving system and window seat, thus creating another focal point in the room. With this simple concept in place the wall begins to explode with

OPPOSITE: Photographs were taken of every room onto which ideas could be sketched with a felt-tip pen.

THE SEVEN LAYERS

LAYER 1: PAINT AND ARCHITECTURE
After installing our architectural window bench and ledges, we combined three dramatic colors—deep plum, dusty green, and chocolate brown. We took care to mix these colors evenly around the room for visual balance.

LAYER 2: INSTALLED FLOORING
We chose a neutral cream color for our wall-to-wall carpet, planning to cover it with an area rug later. Although we chose the carpet at this stage, we delayed the installation until the painting and construction were finished.

LAYER 3: HIGH-TICKET UPHOLSTERY
You will note that we visually tied the club chairs together by interchanging the back pillows. Club chairs and ottomans provided better and more versatile seating than sofas.

LAYER 4: ACCENT FABRICS
We loved the monochromatic feel of the room, so we retained the palette at the window by using a Roman shade in muted tones. Busier fabrics and colors would have robbed the space of its modern feeling.

LAYER 5: NONUPHOLSTERED SURFACES
When in doubt go big with the coffee table. We also added a matching side table. Storage in the kitchen room divider and the window bench helped keep clutter to a minimum.

LAYER 6: ACCESSORIES
To unite the elements of the room with a modern flair, we featured all black-and-white photography by Douglas Hill. As the jewelry of the room, chrome accessories were hip, yet traditional in line.

LAYER 7: PLANTS AND LIGHTING
A simple coffee table plant was all this room needed. But it was the accent lighting and stylish lamp bases that illuminated the room to its best.

"Modern doesn't have to mean stark or cold. Rich background color, simple unadorned furniture, and accessories make a room more tailored and thus more contemporary."

possibilities: It now has a merchandising ledge overhead, and it has storage boxes on each side, two built-in side tables, and an upholstered bench, under which we could create lots of space for storing those things we need only for special occasions. And all within a very small footprint. How cool is that?

Triple thicknesses of MDF (Medium Density Fiberboard—you're going to hear me talk about this versatile material a lot) were used between the storage boxes on each side of the window to mimic the mass of the fireplace mantel. Another shelf above the fireplace lines up exactly with the shelves in the room divider. We also installed purchased shelves on the wall between the new modular unit and the fireplace and beyond, connecting the horizontal line all the way around the room.

Then we tackled the fireplace. It was so out of scale to this little space, we knew we had to do something to bring it into perspective. The Japanese are absolute masters when it comes to dealing with small spaces, so who better to borrow a few ideas from? Over hundreds of years they have developed a system for creating the illusion of depth where there is virtually none. But Japanese design is not just about physical size, it's about how the objects are arranged in layers, kind of like my Seven Layers of Design.

Everywhere you look in a traditional Japanese house or garden you will find a foreground, middle ground, and background, which allows you to enjoy what you see slowly. With that in mind, the shelving we installed on either side of the fireplace was merchandised to become the

OPPOSITE: The built-in window seat will afford more room for guests at your next party and can be a great place to curl up with a good book.

During

ABOVE LEFT: Simply framed photographs can be an inexpensive way to accessorize.
ABOVE RIGHT: Shelving gives lots of opportunities for merchandising your favorite objects, while adding color and texture to the room.
BELOW: Because they have hidden brackets and can be primed or painted any color, these shelves from IKEA are versatile enough to go just about anywhere.

background. By limiting the color palette to rich browns, black, and silver, the overall effect remained unified and kept the space from breaking up into a jumble. This merchandising was carried across the existing mantel, over which a second shelf had been installed to place more objects, thus unifying the entire wall. Now the fireplace visually recedes, instead of dominating the space like the elephant in the middle of the room everyone's afraid of bumping into.

A general rule of thumb is that club chairs placed side by side are a more flexible solution in small spaces than a love seat. Each person has a defined seating space, and chairs are more portable. To maximize seating in the foreground, we placed two curvaceous club chairs in a geometric print on each side of the window, angled in to the large center coffee table. Everything is at arm's length, and everyone seated in the room has access to this table. If you were to look at the furniture layout from above, you would see that by rotating the chairs forty-five degrees from the angles of the walls, we gained a lot of space around each chair, leaving us more room to bring in even more seating. It's a principle we were able to put to effective use in our Traditional living room next door as well.

You'll notice the coffee table has a second shelf below that is a perfect place to stack books or magazines (neatly, please), freeing up the table's top for sculptural accents. We think that's terrific. On the other side of the coffee table, we put two more club chairs. They are in the same design but the fabric is striped;

we cross-pollinated their colors by simply changing the pillows. The chairs gave us just enough room on both sides of the fireplace niche to put two identical coffee tables and a pair of identical lamps. These tables and lamps and a few carefully chosen objects provide the middle ground we needed to transition visually from the foreground seating area to the background shelving. That gives the room a powerful sense of symmetry. We threw in an ottoman opposite the fireplace and voilà! In one small space we had comfortable seating for six! When we first looked at the room, we were challenged to find room even for four.

Chrome accessories distributed around the space bring jewelry accents to the room. Nature-inspired black-and-white photographs against celadon and dusty mauve background colors bring the walls and ledges alive. Incidentally, when we first put up those colors they looked interesting all by themselves. But now that we have placed everything into the room, those colors have become the background that has helped the accessories and furniture really pop. It's the Seven Layers of Design at work again. Even though the big bay window lets in plenty of sunlight to grow beautifully healthy plants, we decided to go with the maintenance-free artificial variety. The technology has come such a long way, nobody can tell the difference.

Our first dreamscape is complete. You will find that once you come up with a concept, the rest falls into place. You start with that core idea, you understand why you are attracted to it, and then you figure out a way to bring your idea into three-dimensional existence. That's how dreamscaping works. When you have the courage to get over certain dilemmas and push your dream forward, you'll experience the adrenaline rush that comes from watching family and friends as they witness this amazing transformation for the first time. You'll get so hooked on the process you'll start dreaming about what you can do in the other rooms of your house. And that's the whole idea.

ABOVE: Good merchandising helps to visually bridge the living room and the kitchen beyond.

Club Chairs, *Not* Sofas or Love Seats

HERE'S a riddle: How many strangers can comfortably sit on a love seat? Unless you want to force folks to get to know each other a lot better really fast, maximum occupancy of your standard-issue love seat is one. I know you knew that.

When you think about it, the footprint of a love seat takes up a lot of precious real estate in a room, especially if it's a small space. And when only one person can sit on it, you're limiting your options considerably.

So instead of a love seat, why not try using two comfortable upholstered chairs. Each person will have his or her own space without feeling cramped. When you are entertaining large groups, the arm of an upholstered chair might become a seat, provided the occupant of the chair is okay with the arrangement. Individual chairs can also be easily angled in any direction to facilitate conversation or traffic flow. And if you need to move one seat into a different room, it's a lot simpler than sawing a love seat in two.

Between the chairs I often place a couple of pedestals or a side table. Now the arrangement allows for placement of a lamp, a tchotchke, or, more important, beverages and serving dishes. While you're at it, pieces with even small drawers become indispensable for storing coasters and napkins.

Ottomans placed side by side can be another flexible seating option. Remember, whenever you add a tray to an ottoman, it becomes a workhorse, too. Love that dual functionality. Witness Layer 5 at work.

A backless settee can also serve as the cross-linking piece between conversation groupings. Your friends can sit on either side of the settee and enjoy the view of a fireplace or window or talk with guests seated across from them.

Keep rooms flexible and multifunctional by making wise furniture choices that offer the greatest variety of seating options.

RIGHT: Club chairs and ottomans are more versatile than a sofa and can actually seat more people comfortably.

traditional living room

OPEN KITCHEN, open dining room, open living room. Open spaces may sound like a terrific idea; however, as we'll see, they can be a very common problem in a lot of the newer homes. How on earth do you treat these wide-open spaces?

As in our Modern living room, we found an object that set the tone for this Traditional living room, in this case a small ceramic container. It has an interesting shape and is deco-

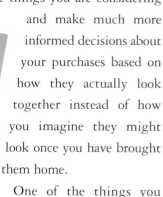

rated in an Asian motif, suggesting a timeless simplicity. And just as important, it is finished in colors we thought would be interesting to work with on the walls, in the fabrics, and in every other element of the room. It is easy to shop if you carry your icon (or a photograph of it if it's too big) along with you to the store. That way you can hold it right up to the things you are considering and make much more informed decisions about your purchases based on how they actually look together instead of how you imagine they might look once you have brought them home.

One of the things you really have to consider in open spaces is traffic patterns. In the Traditional house we

THE SEVEN LAYERS

LAYER 1: PAINT AND ARCHITECTURE
We painted this room in three dramatic colors. Because of the vaulted ceiling, we added a piece of molding at the 8-foot mark all around the room. This gave us a place to stop and start color. From the molding up we painted our ceiling color. From the molding down, we painted one of our wall colors. (Tip: If you introduce more than one wall color, be sure to balance that color evenly throughout the space.)

LAYER 2: INSTALLED FLOORING
We started with plywood floors and had the choice of adding wall-to-wall carpet. We chose a cream color for the entire space to help unite the dining room, living room, and kitchen. (We chose the carpet at this stage but decided to install it after all painting and construction were finished.)

LAYER 3: HIGH-TICKET UPHOLSTERY
We knew club chairs and ottomans were the way to go. Because we knew they could be moved into any room, we were more aggressive with the fabric. But still we kept the fabric free of aggressive pattern.

LAYER 4: ACCENT FABRICS
Using throw pillows and generous panels at the window, we chose accent fabrics that could be inexpensively changed according to the season or if it was time for a new look. We laid an area rug over the wall-to-wall to add detail underfoot and define the conversational space.

LAYER 5: NONUPHOLSTERED SURFACES
The table between the club chairs and the oversize coffee table assured that a surface was comfortably at arm's length. The tonsu-style room divider gave us extra storage for books and accessories. The wooden settee was a cross-linking device to separate one room from the other. It also served for both additional seating and storage.

LAYER 6: ACCESSORIES
Because of the small space, we kept accessories to a minimum and focused instead on large-scale pieces united by similar color.

LAYER 7: PLANTS AND LIGHTING
Topiary at the fireplace added a fresh feeling to the room. When accented with uplights, a focal-point orchid cast great shadows on the wall. Task lamps were placed conveniently by chairs for reading on a high setting or for mood lighting on a low setting.

> "Traditional doesn't have to be stuffy or old-fashioned. Think texture and geometric rather than prints. Your Traditional room will remain timeless."

had a hallway connecting to back bedrooms and a bathroom and another hallway connecting to a master bedroom. And we also had to keep in mind the need to get in and around the kitchen.

To define the living room, we began by constructing a tonsu-style storage unit about 4 feet high and placed it perpendicular to the wall near the front door. It creates an entry corridor we desperately needed and a wall against which we could anchor furniture.

I like to think of furniture placement as conversation islands adrift in the center of high-traffic areas, so we positioned a burgundy-colored ottoman next to the tonsu and placed another ottoman, leaving enough space to include one of a pair of striped club chairs. These transition pieces are easy to navigate around and provide seating for one person. With a tea tray on top, the ottoman can also serve as a coffee table for our nearby cross-linking device. Whenever you can assign more than one task to a piece of furniture, or any other object, for that matter, you are way ahead of the game in small spaces.

We then placed two matching club chairs in a gold-textured fabric flanking the front window with a full-size end table in between to connect them. Two more club chairs were placed on the other side of the fireplace with the ottoman we already had in position between them. The chairs are identical to the gold ones, but we gave them a whole new attitude

OPPOSITE: An oversize coffee table placed in front of the fireplace services all seating.

merely by changing their fabric to a lush green, gold, and purple. Now, look at the floor. We laid this Oriental rug right over the house's wall-to-wall carpet. Its muted colors go perfectly with our overall scheme and add yet another layer of texture to the space. The oversize coffee table placed in front of the fireplace is large enough to service all seating. On top of it we placed lots of candles of different colors and heights, stressing the importance of high/low when it comes to displays. What is high/low? Ever look at a great city skyline? There are short buildings and skyscrapers and all sorts of levels in between that allow you to see far more of the city than you would if they were all the same height. The same is true of arranging things like candles, or anything else you might want to decorate a horizontal surface with. Take a tip from the city: Give your displays variety and the eye will never get bored.

The same principle was applied to the fireplace, only this time in a powerful symmetrical fashion. Tightly cropped topiary trees with long trunks were placed on the floor on either side, while matching vases exploding with fluffy red flowers went onto the mantel astride an

RIGHT: To define the living room, we began by constructing a tonsu-style storage unit about 4 feet high placed perpendicular to the wall near the front door. It creates an entry corridor and a wall against which we could put furniture.

The Cross-Linking Device

SO MANY smaller houses being built today feature open spaces. It is impossible to tell where one "room" ends and another "room" begins. The result can leave one with an uncomfortable sense of chaos. What is needed are clear definition, visual anchors, and focal points. This is where the cross-linking device comes in. Barriers are necessary, so that the space is not revealed all at once. The ideal cross-linking device is one that provides functionality to each of the rooms it's called upon to help define while turning its back on none of them. In fact, cross-linking devices have no backs. They can be appreciated from all angles since they are usually freestanding or jut out from a wall into the space like the architectural equivalent of a peninsula. They can incorporate storage (always a great idea in a volume-challenged home) either visible or hidden, provide seating (something else you can't have too much of), or simply be a fabulous object to look at. If a cross-linking device boasts all three, you have got something special. Just make sure this critical piece doesn't disrupt the necessary flow of traffic, and you can't go wrong.

understated abstract print. Of course, the nice thing about flowers is that they are an element you can switch on a whim. You can either use the dried kind, as we did here, or replace them with the real thing whenever the mood for change strikes you. (Just make sure your containers are designed to hold water.) The tied-back window treatment behind the matching gold club chairs created a sense of the orderliness that allowed us to play much more freely with the arrangement on the coffee table. Although the resulting mood is very different from the one we created in our Modern living room, we have effectively layered the space in the same way. The Traditional living room has the illusion of depth.

On the opposite side of the room, beyond the pass-through to the bedrooms, we built a cross-linking device. It's a simple settee, really, made of two plywood boxes connected by an upholstered seat and a lower ledge for storage. (See page 127 for building instructions.) Simple. But with just the right merchandising it becomes chic as well as functional. While it is low enough to see over, it is also narrow enough to leave pass-through space on either side and links one cluster area with another. With two large Kentia palms placed on the top ledges, it really illustrates the point that foliage adds amazing height and drama to a room, dividing the spaces with just a tropical touch. Of course, if you would rather not build one, you can create the same effect by purchasing a backless settee—just add a couple of pedestals or cubbies to support the necessary foliage. Whichever way you decide to go, a cross-linking device such as this can beautifully delineate what started out as one big space into true living and dining rooms without cramping the style of either one. In fact, I think our cross-linking device has truly become the focal point of both rooms. At the same time there is now additional seating in both. We have effectively increased the seating capacity of the living room to a remarkable eight.

Something to keep in mind when it comes to furniture placement: Lay it out in advance before you actually purchase your furniture. Take into consideration all conversation clusters and entryways. And remember, for passageways: The human form needs 18 inches to navigate. A well-thought-out plan will keep you from inadvertently creating spatial cul-de-sacs and save you lots of money in the future, not to mention bruised shins. Ouch!

OPPOSITE: This settee we built works beautifully to delineate what was at first one big space into the living room and dining room. With two large Kentia palms placed on the top ledges, it really illustrates the point that foliage adds amazing height and drama to a room, dividing the spaces with just a tropical touch.

2

finite
foyers

divide-and-conquer foyer

SO HERE'S A CHALLENGE: a big open space with a front door smack in the middle of the room so you kind of just fall right in. There are also two totally undefined seating areas in the middle of a high-traffic speedway. Are we having fun yet?

On the right as you enter a fireplace sits along the wall. I guess that area is intended to be the living room. To the left of the door there's more space, which, if I'm reading the floor plan correctly, is supposed to  be used as a den. In front of the door we have what home builders like to call a foyer: floor tile laid out 3 feet by 3 feet. Hmmm. Pretty appealing, huh? Alrighty then, let's roll up our sleeves.

Remember that in design we always talk about how much more interesting rooms are when you have to walk around things, and the room is revealed slowly. Love that. So we began by building a series of boxes, floor to ceiling, separated by three shelves made with a triple thickness of MDF (Medium Density Fiberboard). (See page 43 for building instructions.) A column was placed perpendicular to the wall next to the floor tile and extended out into the room almost to the edge of the tile.

Painted a soft celadon color to match the fireplace, the column blends into the background and sets off the foyer as a defined space. The dusty mauve wall color of the living room provides the background to the chocolate-colored shelving accessorized by black-and-white nature-inspired photos. Large tchotchkes placed on the divider shelves help

THE SEVEN LAYERS

LAYER 1: PAINT AND ARCHITECTURE
The unit we built, a movable room divider, was the perfect embellishment *and* served dual functions: It added not only architecture but also storage (Layer 5). Since this space was part of two other rooms we kept to the same color scheme.

LAYER 2: INSTALLED FLOORING
The small tiled entry was already gray, so we simply matched it to the wall-to-wall carpet to be installed after all painting and construction were finished.

LAYER 3: HIGH-TICKET UPHOLSTERY
The only time upholstery will be part of this space is when the ottomans from the den are removed, so that the sofa has room to fold out into a bed.

LAYER 4: ACCENT FABRICS
We did add accent fabric in this small windowless foyer—but only its reflection in a mirror that showed up in Layer 6. It reflected the great upholstered pieces in the entire room. Cool!

LAYER 5: NONUPHOLSTERED SURFACES
We added a hall demitable to the existing divider we made in Layer 1. It's a great place to throw the car keys.

LAYER 6: ACCESSORIES
Once it was accented with great decorative pieces, the dividing unit really made sense. The mirror, placed on the floor, visually opened up the space and reflected the entire living room. I love mirror magic.

LAYER 7: PLANTS AND LIGHTING
A large tree, uplit, cast shadows on the rich wall color and made for a warm and inviting first impression.

BELOW: As a plywood alternative, MDF (Medium Density Fiberboard) is used liberally for all sorts of interior projects.

theme the space, while giving the divider greater impact. A niche area between the new divider and the fireplace is now the perfect spot for a side table that accompanies one of the club chairs in the living room and gives balance to a similar area on the far side of the fireplace. What began as a kind of creepy little corner is now valuable, attractive living space. The divider also addresses much needed storage. Very cool.

Now, when you walk in the front door, you are greeted by a well-defined, attractive architectural interruption that adds a bit of mystery to what might be in the house beyond. And while you and your friends are sitting in the living room enjoying the fireplace and each other's company, you don't have to stare at the front door waiting for the rest of your guests to arrive.

Don't worry, we haven't forgotten about the left side of the entry. You know, that empty space where the den is supposed to be? We built a horizontal header, or false beam, below the vaulted ceiling and installed incredibly versatile SpaceXDoors. These units are floor-to-ceiling bookcases on one side and solid walls on the other that move along a track and fold together, providing an open or closed option to form a wall. Isn't that cool? We'll see them again in chapter 8 (see pages 150–152).

We decided that since the SpaceXDoors left a more than generous opening on the far side that we would leave the bookcase/"walls" next to the entry permanently closed. This gave us a wonderful opportunity to put an oversize mirror up against the back of the shelves. This technique is used in a lot of very chic hotels, and it works great right here in our small space. The mirror is just set on the floor, leaning up against the wall, with a little demitable in front of it. It reflects the entire length of the living room and eliminates the claustrophobic feeling. A tall artificial floor plant helps soften the archway going around the corner to what will soon be much more than your average den, and with an uplight underneath, showcases a little bit of

"The illusion of space is the next best thing to having it."

OPPOSITE: The mirror now reflects the entire length of the living room and eliminates the claustrophobic feeling. A tall artificial floor plant helps soften the archway going around the corner to the library, and with an uplight underneath, showcases a little bit of shadow on the wall. I think that looks great.

During

ABOVE: A niche between the new divider and the fireplace is now the perfect spot for a side table that accompanies one of the club chairs in the living room. What was a useless corner is now valuable living space that also addresses much-needed storage. Very cool.

shadow on the wall. I think that looks great. Mirror magic can cast a whole new reflection on your room.

So if you find yourself in a situation where you open the door and it's just sort of "do drop in anytime," try interrupting the space to maximize the space. It creates unity, but more important, it creates division. The living room is now a livable room, while the den, with retractable doors and the addition of a foldout couch, can double as a den-library by day and a guest bedroom by night. Love that double, excuse me, triple duty. Don't you?

foyer divider

materials

¾-inch sheets MDF (Medium
   Density Fiberboard) or plywood

Wood glue

Clamps

Wood screws

Wood veneer

Finishing nails

Table saw

Power drill and screwdriver

Hammer

Tape measure

Level

Safety glasses

Wood putty

Sandpaper

Wood primer and brush

Paint and paintbrushes

① For the base, construct a rectangular four-sided box using ¾-inch MDF or plywood at counter height.

② Each shelf is constructed of 3 thicknesses of ¾-inch MDF or plywood. Apply wood glue to the surfaces of the shelving boards, stack 3 of them together, and clamp in place. Screw the shelves together along the ends. Let dry. Cut wood veneer for the edges of the shelves, glue to the edges, and attach with finishing nails.

③ Build four-sided square boxes the desired height for the upright supports. Glue and screw the 4 sides together. Measure the inner dimensions of the opening of the upright columns and cut squares of ¾-inch MDF or plywood for the top and bottom of each column. These wood blocks will secure the columns to the shelves, locking them into place.

④ Secure wood blocks to the top and underside at one end of each shelf. Attach one shelf to the top of the base. Place an upright support over the wood block on the top of the shelf and secure with screws.

⑤ Add another shelf, placing the wood block on the underside over the opening at the top of the upright support. At the other end of the shelf, place a wood brace along the wall between the 2 shelves.

Keep stacking shelves and supports to the desired height of the divider. Fill in nail and screw holes with wood putty. Sand, prime with a stain-blocking primer, and paint.

free-floating entry

I HEAR PEOPLE SAY ALL THE TIME, "I fall into my living room. There's no mystery." Good design is about mystery. Rooms are much more interesting when they take some time to enter. So how do you create mystery in a "tell-all" space?

In our Traditional living room we were presented with an off-center fireplace, a double window on the adjacent wall, and a front door way over in the corner with no space between itself and the side wall. Let's not even mention that this space is also opposite the dining area and two halls leading in opposite directions. It's like a roller rink. Oh, brother! What we needed was something to define where the living room begins and where a foyer should live. In some cases, just a simple sofa placement where the back of the sofa creates a corridor might work. But we really don't think sofas are such a great idea in these smaller spaces, and they're certainly not tall enough to visually break up the space, so we decided to create what we like to call a free-floating visible barrier. Think of it as something that you know is there, so it defines a space but allows enough opportunity to see over, around, or through it to keep you from feeling claustrophobic.

We built a freestanding two-tiered shelving unit with lots of cubbyholes for storage. The height was slightly above waist level, and the construction was symmetrical with three cubbies on top centered over five on the bottom. Then we pushed it around the room for a while to find its best

THE SEVEN LAYERS

LAYER 1: PAINT AND ARCHITECTURE
The built-in tonsu was a godsend; it supplied not only an element of architecture to the space but also storage. And it is a great device for defining a new entry. We used the same colors as in the rest of the room (see "Traditional Living Room," page 28).

LAYER 2: INSTALLED FLOORING
The wall-to-wall carpet used in the entire open space had to match the few floor tiles at the front door, so we kept it simple.

LAYER 3: HIGH-TICKET UPHOLSTERY
With no room for upholstery, we decided to reflect it from the living room, with the mirror that we added in Layer 6.

LAYER 4: ACCENT FABRICS
Once again, we decided to let a mirror reflect our accent fabrics. We thought of adding a runner to our new foyer floor, but we would have had to shave off too much of the front door. So we settled for an area rug in the living room placed on top of the wall-to-wall carpet.

LAYER 5: NONUPHOLSTERED SURFACES
Our new tonsu divider not only gave us a movable space planner but also contained storage and ledges ready for Layer 6.

LAYER 6: ACCESSORIES
We added that wonderful mirror flanked by prints to bring interest to the foyer. Books and objects on the tonsu help merchandise it and integrate it into the living room. The rest of the minifoyer we left clean and clutter-free for better traffic control.

LAYER 7: PLANTS AND LIGHTING
A few orchid plants gave life to our room divider. Lamps provided a warm and cozy illumination to our new entryway.

During

Tips for False Visible Barriers

REMEMBER, first impressions make the greatest lasting impact. Whether you live in an apartment or a house, the very first thing your guests see when you open the front door for them is your entryway. Therefore, it's important to ask yourself, "Does my entry project a sense of grandeur, or is it merely a pass-through space? Does it exist at all?"

If people are standing in your living room the second they step through your front door, you can create what I refer to as a false visible barrier to separate the entryway from the living space. In our Modern home, we built a shelving unit from floor to ceiling that was placed perpendicular to the edge of the door. With tchotchkes placed on the shelves you could just barely see the living room beyond, but at the same time didn't feel entirely cut off from it, either.

In our Traditional home, a counter-high tonsu created the illusion of a hallway, directing traffic either into the living room or toward the dining room. A grand-scale mirror and artwork on the wall completed the hallway illusion.

If you are not handy with a hammer and saw, try using a purchased bookcase with the back placed opposite the front door. Finish the back, or upholster it with fabric and hang a mirror or framed pictures on it to create a false wall. (Make sure the back of the piece is strong enough to support these accessories before you buy it.) You will also gain lots of great storage on the other side.

Other options to consider are a swing-out curtain rod with luxurious shirred fabric tied back to the wall with wonderful tassels to create softness, and folding screens that you can cover with a fabric in your color scheme.

ABOVE: Here the entry is already beginning to look more like a real foyer . . . and we're not even finished. We have a runner for the floor and art still to put up.

placement. We figured if we placed our shelving unit up against the front wall in typical tonsu fashion it would make the doorway seem cramped and the room feel out of proportion. So it was pulled out into the room and positioned opposite the fireplace. It still created a corridor and walkway area, but it also gave us the option of directly entering the living room by walking around either side of the unit. Since the fireplace was going to be our focal point, this position added spatial balance to the room. The unit also gave us another anchor around which to place furniture with confidence. Not bad for an object with such humble origins. It just goes to show how much can be accomplished with simple construction and some paint.

So what about furniture placement? This room was so small even love seats weren't practical, and you know how I feel about love seats anyway. The best solution for flexible seating in the adjacent living room was club chairs. They could be angled into the room to maximize space as well as leave plenty of room to move around them. With that decision in mind, we decided to face the cubbyhole side of our new unit into the living room. With two chairs flanking both sides and a low ottoman in front, storage of books and magazines that otherwise make a living room look really cluttered was accessible from the inside of the room. Merchandising ledges gave us the opportunity to add accessories, plants, and a bit of mood lighting. And since nothing had to be bolted down, it allowed us to play around with different sizes and shapes of objects to give our room divider just the right scale and texture.

In order to retrieve some of the visual space that we lost to our shelving unit, we added a framed mirror to the side wall that's big enough to reach nearly floor to ceiling. It almost suggests another doorway and a room beyond. So now, when you walk

"Rooms need a bit of mystery. Don't reveal all, at least not all at once."

in, you see the actual room and the reflection of the room in the mirror on the other side. Two for the price of one! I love a good mirror. Once again employing the power of symmetry, we flanked the mirror with a pair of large framed prints to finish the look. Most important, this space is now very well defined.

Oh yeah, the drop-dead wall color didn't hurt, either. It proves that rich, juicy color does just fine in smaller spaces! Who knew?

During

RIGHT: We built a freestanding two-tiered shelving unit with lots of cubbyholes for storage. The height was slightly above waist level, and the construction was symmetrical with three cubbies on top centered over five on the bottom. Then we pushed it around the room for a while to find its best placement.

3

mini
master
suites

south seas zen bedroom

WHEN I THINK OF A PAMPERING SPACE, the icon word for me is *retreat*. And one of my favorite themes is the Balinese look. But can windswept tropical nights fit into a 10-by-10-foot space? Or is the reality simply a typhoon out of control? As I have said before, you start and you end your day here, so make the most of it. When you walk into a space like this, think of it as a creative canvas just waiting to have your ideas applied to it.

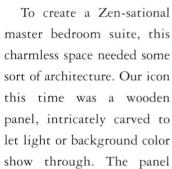

To create a Zen-sational master bedroom suite, this charmless space needed some sort of architecture. Our icon this time was a wooden panel, intricately carved to let light or background color show through. The panel reinforced our Balinese theme and suggested a terrific idea for another decorative element. Lengths of board mounted vertically and horizontally could create a tracery effect on the walls not unlike the carving in our wood panel. We decided to use low-grade pine for budgetary reasons, but its naturally distressed look actually helped achieve the look we were going for. Before putting the boards up we aged the wood even further by faux-finishing it in a rust-colored base coat, then adding a lighter green on top and randomly sanding, so the two colors showed through. (See page 56 for technique instructions.) What a concept! It added a lot of organic texture to the room and really

(See page 56 for technique instructions.)

THE SEVEN LAYERS

LAYER 1: PAINT AND ARCHITECTURE
We love the vertical and horizontal drama created by applying strips of faux-finished pine. We painted the walls and ceiling first, then applied the finished architecture. More detail would be added later in Layer 6. Bamboo placed in openings and used as a suspended canopy over the bed would be the theme here.

LAYER 2: INSTALLED FLOORING
We chose a neutral wall-to-wall carpet knowing we were going to add an area rug later. Because it was new construction, we delayed the installation of the carpet until the paint and wood-work were complete.

LAYER 3: HIGH-TICKET UPHOLSTERY
When dealing with a bedroom, the actual bed is classified as the upholstered focal point, but the same principles apply as in any other room. Keep your comforters and bed linens neutral. Rule of thumb: luxurious enough for her, tailored enough for him!

LAYER 4: ACCENT FABRICS
We added decorative window panels with sheer inserts in a leaf motif. Accent pillows added sheen and a feeling of luxury to the room. They were also placed on the bamboo bench. How chic. Our miniblinds became accents once we sprayed them cinnabar. The sea grass rug under the bed helped continue our organic theme underfoot.

LAYER 5: NONUPHOLSTERED SURFACES
The overscale bedside tables added storage and function on either side of the bed. But it was the large chest that really made the room not only practical but also better in balance and scale because it was built up right to the window.

LAYER 6: ACCESSORIES
We clustered our accessories into vignettes and used color to unite them. Distressed wall pieces helped add an aura of antiquity to the space. When a theme is well defined, shopping for accessories to merchandise your space is a breeze.

LAYER 7: PLANTS AND LIGHTING
Uplights shining through the tropical palm trees added an exotic feeling to the space. Its shadows provided a romantic feeling amplified by the flicker of candlelight. Oversize lamps also helped play up the global feeling we were trying to achieve.

played up the intricacies of the woodwork. Using intentionally primitive materials costs much less. Not only that, the more rustic a piece is, the more forgiving it is when it comes to installation. If it's slightly askew or off-center, it just looks like it was meant to be that way.

Nevertheless, the arrangement of boards was carefully laid out beforehand to assure that the wood didn't cover essential switches or wall plugs. We did want to be able to turn the lights off and on, you know. By treating just the walls in such a fashion, our master bedroom was already completely transformed with nothing in it. Another bonus was that the ceiling now had the appearance of having been set in. How can you beat that? Moving right along!

Fueled by great results, we turned our attentions to the real focus and theme of this room—the bed. How big is too big? Well, we don't call it a BEDroom for nothing, do we? So why not really play it up. We began with the base, creating a floating platform out of simple MDF. We extended out the base much farther than the mattress, which provided a ledge that visually lifts the bed off the ground and gives it a minimal, exotic feeling. Since the window above it seemed out of scale, we simply incorporated it into the headboard and canopy.

The canopy was made by overlapping large bamboo pieces, tying them in a latticework motif with good old hemp rope, then suspending the canopy from the vaulted ceiling with garden pot hooks. (For obvious reasons we made sure the hooks and all our ties were absolutely secure before we went any further!) Then it was time to fluff. The same fabric was used in the drapes hung directly from the canopy and for the bed coverings. Inspired by the papers that line the inside of Chinese boxes, the iridescent fabric allows filtered light to come through its

TOP, LEFT TO RIGHT: Within a day of installation, the room's shell was already completely transformed with nothing in it. **LEFT:** Still life is very important. From the primitive artifacts to the crackle-finished mirror to the corbels and plants, everything is poetic, simple, and chic. A bamboo bench and some of the matching pillows from the bed bring the fabric pattern over to that side of the room.

paint technique: block aging

materials

Wood mirror or picture frame

6-inch 2-by-4 piece of wood

4-inch 1-by-2 piece of wood

Latex paint:

   Base coat color (we used white)

   Aging color #1 (we used medium gray)

   Aging color #2 (we used light gray)

   Aging color #3 (we used sage green)

Sandpaper

Paintbrushes

Painter's blue tape

Tack cloth

1 Sand and prepare the surface of the wood mirror or frame. Paint the entire frame with the base coat color and let dry.

2 Tape off the corners to represent miter cuts diagonally from the inner corner to the outer corner of the frame.

3 Dip a paintbrush sparingly into aging color #1 and brush it onto the 4-inch surface of the 2-by-4 piece of wood.

4 Scuff the painted side of the block over the base coat of the frame, hitting and slightly dragging the paint over the wood until small amounts of the aging color are left on the surface. Be sure to follow the natural grain of the wood. Repeat until the desired effect is achieved.

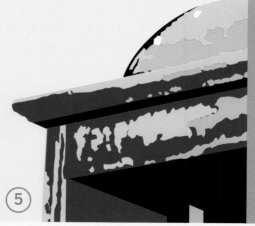

5 Dip a paintbrush sparingly into aging color #2 and brush it onto the 2-inch surface of the 1-by-2 piece of wood. Apply in the same manner by scuffing and dragging the paint over the wood. Repeat with aging color #3. If you feel you have added too much color, dip the paintbrush into the base coat color and stipple over the aging colors.

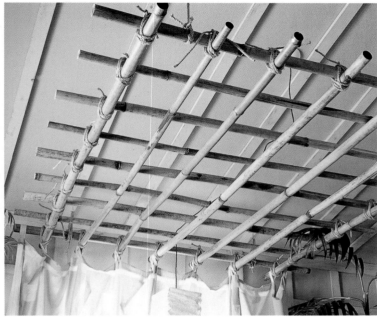

sheer, leaf pattern blocks during the day, adding to the room's organic feeling. By using the bed to determine the width of the drapes we effectively disguised the size of the window behind them, making them feel larger.

To elongate the whole bed unit, we added square tea tables beautifully accessorized with two matching lamps in a primitive motif as well. Continuing the symmetry, we added big Kentia palms with uplights behind that cast those mysterious, intimate shadows. That completed the bed ensemble.

To balance out the scale of the new bed, the large double window along the far wall had to be built up as well. We found a wooden chest at a store and completely reworked it with new textural elements. Bamboo panels and pine lathing strips attached to the individual drawers, on top of which were mounted brass pulls, make the chest look hundreds of years old, which in a piece like this is good. No, really. With a little elbow grease and not much money, we turned an unfinished chest into an heirloom. We love that. We had considered the idea of replacing the miniblinds that came with the house with rice-paper shades, but the effect was too high-key. Then we thought about plantation shutters, but they were way too thick. So we threw up our hands and painted the original miniblinds the same rust color that we used to treat the pine tracery, thus tying them in to the look of the room. And they were just right. An added bonus we couldn't have foreseen is that when partially open, the blinds also cast an amazing light onto the top of the chest and give the celadon, dark wood, and white-crackle-finished objects we placed on

ABOVE, LEFT AND RIGHT: The canopy was made by weaving large bamboo pieces together, tying them in a latticework motif with good old hemp rope, then suspending the canopy from the vaulted ceiling with garden pot hooks.

"Don't panic with a large bed in a small space. It's a focal point. So play it up!"

it a warm, ethereal glow. You just never quite know what will happen until it is all put together.

Still life becomes very important on the wall facing the foot of the bed. From the primitive artifacts to the crackle-finished mirror to the corbels and plants, everything here is poetic, simple, and chic. A bamboo bench and some of the matching pillows from the bed bring the fabric pattern over to that side of the room.

RIGHT: Then it was time to fluff. The fabric in the drapes matches the pattern in the bed coverings. Inspired by the papers that line the inside of Chinese boxes, the iridescent fabric allows filtered light to come through, adding to the room's organic feeling.

bali bathroom

WHEN WE THINK OF CREATING a bathroom with a meditative quality to it, we think of the luxurious resort spas, places where those with the means can have their every healthful whim indulged. Massages, mud baths, and facials all day long may be very nice, but they are not practical for most busy, everyday lives. However, we can allow ourselves access to an environment that is conducive to the same kind of serenity. It won't cost you a fortune, since it's going to be in your own home. I'm thinking fluffy white terry-cloth robes. I'm thinking slippers and lots of scented decorative candles. I'm thinking wonderful toiletry containers to hold the products we enjoy without company logos staring us in the face. I'm thinking texture and mood everywhere you look. I'm thinking it's something you and I deserve and need to treat ourselves to on a regular basis for true peace of mind. Are you with me?

We liked the blood pressure–reducing bamboo theme in the bedroom so much that we decided to continue it through into the adjoining master bath. We accomplished this by building an archway over the entry to the vanity area, which had originally been way taller than we needed it to be, and vertically hanging lengths of bamboo from the header. We also replaced the less-than-exotic etched-glass divider into the bath with more bamboo trim. It's organic. It's textural. The light streams through it in all sorts of interesting patterns, and now the two rooms feel connected like never before. Isn't it also remarkable what a little bit of

THE SEVEN LAYERS

LAYER 1: PAINT AND ARCHITECTURE
The key to a successful master bath is to follow the bedroom theme into this space with both color and embellishments. The same applied molding was added here and a deep rust color in the tub area pulled the eye through the space. Bamboo bars in the opening helped continue our bamboo accent between spaces.

LAYER 2: INSTALLED FLOORING
The sink area introduced the vinyl floor. It matched the color of the master bedroom's wall-to-wall carpet. Remember to keep these surfaces neutral.

LAYER 3: HIGH-TICKET UPHOLSTERY
There was no room for upholstery. (But in larger baths, I love an ottoman to sit on while toweling off after a hot shower.)

LAYER 4: ACCENT FABRICS
Simple colored towels can really do the trick. We even have them rolled in baskets overhead as well as on the bamboo floor rack. The shower curtain is also a good place to showcase an accent fabric, as long as it's used with a plastic liner for protection.

LAYER 5: NONUPHOLSTERED SURFACES
The sink cabinet is the only surface, but because it's built into the structure, it is added in Layer 1. Again, keep your surfaces neutral. You'll always be able to merchandise those counters with great bath accessories.

LAYER 6: ACCESSORIES
Speaking of which, we used our small space wisely by organizing spa products and other bath items in decorative containers. This helps stretch the function of the room. The bamboo towel rack continued the organic feeling. Decorative wall pieces also helped play up the global theme from the master bedroom.

LAYER 7: PLANTS AND LIGHTING
Candles are really all you are going to need when you bathe, but you can supplement with strategically directed spots on dimmers and still maintain a high romance quotient. There isn't a lot of room for plants, but the ones to go with are soft, leafy types such as ferns. A bit tropical, a bit Bali.

vibrant wall color will do to make a space feel more accommodating? The light green tracery effect from the bedroom, with its touches of cinnabar, was brought through to underline the unity of the spaces as well. We have created a transition, giving our most private space a sense of expansion in the process.

The faux-finished mossy green laminate vanity countertop came with the house, and at first it looked out of place against the original white walls, but when we surrounded it with another green color and lots of bamboo, it suddenly seemed as if we had chosen it intentionally. Two people have to share this space, so organization is key. Trays and baskets separate his and hers necessities and help unburden existing shelves and cupboards to

OPPOSITE: Two people have to share this space, so organization is key. Trays and baskets separate his and hers necessities and unburden existing shelves.
ABOVE LEFT: Mix and match accessories to take the bathroom from sterile to stellar.

hold what we don't want to have to look at any more than necessary. We even hung baskets from the ceiling to keep scented soaps and candles handy for emergency sensory decompression. You will notice, too, that we didn't flinch at placing seemingly oversize items like the wood candlestick and celadon vase beside the sink, once again proving that small spaces don't require small objects to take on big-time attitude. The distressed tracery in the bathroom, borrowed from the bedroom, turned out to be an inspired move, if we do say so ourselves, giving it architectural detail and a lot of needed character.

A freestanding towel rack with an intricately carved mirror hung above it creates a focal point. As you can see, the towels we have placed throughout are in a medley of rich colors chosen to emphasize the look of the vanity and bath. These small spaces can handle a lot more color than you might think, and there are now so many terrific options out there it doesn't make sense not to take advantage of them. Back in the shower area the same architectural elements, such as plaques on the wall, a deep cinnabar background color, and a great-looking shower curtain, all work together to make the space look warm, cozy, and, more important, pampering. The place is well dressed and well organized. And what about the big bold candlesticks in front of the tub? Those babies actually take up very little footprint, while turning an otherwise drab corner into yet another focal point full of character, drawing the eye from the bedroom into the bathroom. Besides, you can never have too many candles around when it is time to slip into a soothing bath at the end of a long day, as the chrome tea-candle tray on the soap ledge will attest.

Now, the spaces of the master suite that seemed so at odds with each other at first operate as a united front, making the world that much easier for you to face each day. Pardon me if I doze off for a while.

ABOVE: The green laminate countertop looked out of place, but surrounding it with another green color made it seem as if we'd chosen it intentionally. We continued the distressed tracery into the bathroom.
OPPOSITE: A freestanding towel rack with a mirror hung above creates a focal point. The same architectural elements work back in the shower area.

traditional gets innovative

MEANWHILE, back at our Traditional house . . . When we first looked at this room we went into crisis mode. We *hate*—no, I mean *love*—when that happens. Did you know that the word *crisis* in Chinese is made up of the characters for *challenge* and *opportunity*? Me neither. But what a great way to look at things.

Let me explain how this attitude affected our design approach.

First, this room posed a lot of challenges. One entire wall was devoted to closets. Fair enough, we have got to have a place for all our clothes. The adjacent wall had double windows (we need light, too), and there was a great big blank wall on the opposite side. Goody, let's put the bed there. Whoops, that's not possible. See, there's a hallway from the bedroom entry to what will soon become a sunroom. So, if the bed indeed goes up against the wall, then you would have to walk all around it to get from one

LEFT: Try taking a photo and drawing your "after" before you start.
OPPOSITE: Look to nature for color inspiration—love that!

THE SEVEN LAYERS

LAYER 1: PAINT AND ARCHITECTURE
The architectural columns we added to the room started the theme, which we then translated into the bed unit. We added all the heavy construction work first. The paint might have seemed dark initially, but once the space was decorated it became the perfect backdrop.

LAYER 2: INSTALLED FLOORING
We added wall-to-wall carpet first, even though we could have delayed it due to new construction. Because the bed unit would be impossible to move once installed, the wall-to-wall had to be installed first.

LAYER 3: HIGH-TICKET UPHOLSTERY
Treat the bed the same as you would a large sofa in a living room. It's a focal point and an investment. Therefore, focus on textural and solid patterns. We chose a very delicate watercolor-inspired floral. (Tip: If you squint your eyes and it appears to be muted and solid, it will work fine.)

LAYER 4: ACCENT FABRICS
Great pillows on the bed, a throw here or there, and window treatments are all places to add accent fabrics. We decided to use the matching drapes that went with the comforter called Garden Chic, from my home collection.

LAYER 5: NONUPHOLSTERED SURFACES
With so much storage in our island, a small dresser was all that was needed for odds and ends. The bedside tables and shelving were all incorporated into the island bed. How's that for dual function?

LAYER 6: ACCESSORIES
With a traditional garden theme, white crackle-finished items worked well. Wall art helped depict the mood, while larger-scale artifacts helped to merchandise the room appropriately. The great mirror, of course, reflected everything, doubling the magic.

LAYER 7: PLANTS AND LIGHTING
Each of the new columns was ideal for affixing a sconce to accentuate the architecture of the room, while lamps put focused light within arm's reach of the bed. The overhead chandelier added scale, while candles provided romance.

During

"To help theme a room, pick one element and do it en masse."

room to another. I don't think so. Keeping in mind that we had to define this walkway, the only place for the bed was in the middle of the room. That meant there was no space for side tables or other necessary storage. We would have to build a completely self-contained island to solve this crisis. Yeah, sure. That'll work. Well, actually, it does . . . as you will see.

How could you anchor the unit so that it looked, when done, as if it were really part of the intended architecture? We noticed little notches or jogs in two corners of the room built for structure. We decided that what the room needed was country flair. When you think about it, a lot of the old eighteenth-century homes had columns. We incorporated that idea and the jogs became our dream icon.

But we didn't stop at one icon. We had found a cheery blue-and-white planter on one of our hunting-and-gathering trips into which we'd stuck some soft yellow and blue

ABOVE: Keeping it simple can be easy with the right icon. This blue-and-white planter with flowers became the icon for our Traditional master suite, OPPOSITE, suggesting all the colors we would need throughout.

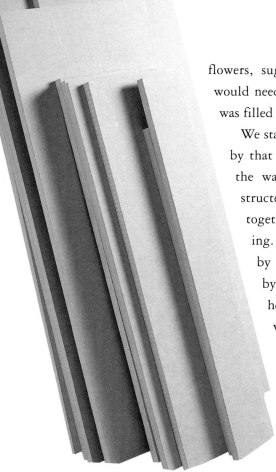

flowers, suggesting virtually all the colors we would need throughout, and suddenly the room was filled with opportunities.

We started by adding false columns, inspired by that little jog I previously mentioned, all the way around the room. They are constructed from three pieces of wood put together and capped off with crown molding. Easy. A center island bed was created by constructing two columns connected by a great big box that forms the bed's headboard, with shelves added to provide plenty of storage. Our platform bed is like a sea captain's bed with the mattress placed on top of our own MDF (Medium Density Fiberboard) box. We also built in an elongated shelf as a nightstand on each side of the bed. It's simple, and we've shown you how to construct it all on page 73.

The bed is played up with a watercolor-inspired comforter that's pretty and soft for her, but tailored enough for him. We used matching curtains on the windows, and to make the windows seem larger, we extended the rod on both

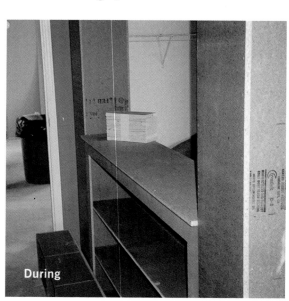

During

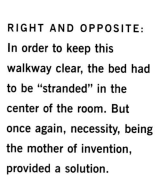

RIGHT AND OPPOSITE: In order to keep this walkway clear, the bed had to be "stranded" in the center of the room. But once again, necessity, being the mother of invention, provided a solution.

"Necessity is the mother of invention— *and* elegance."

sides. Again, it's an opportunity to add more beautiful, soft fabric to what might otherwise have ended up an uncomfortably hard-edged space. We painted the walls a deep, soft blue, and then we painted the ceiling the same color. Very restful. But then, shouldn't a bedroom be designed to promote relaxation?

All this construction and there was still room for a small dresser in the corner. To bring a country-inspired blue to the floor, we added an area rug on top of the wall-to-wall carpet. It grounds the space and gives us something to center the entire bed on. We found elegantly simple matching wall sconces and added one to each of the columns by the bed and around the room. Put them on a dimmer and you've got an instant mood-altering effect. We also removed the track lighting provided with the house and added a fabulous country chandelier. This gives height and scale and is framed perfectly in the mirror that we hung on the wall opposite the opening between the columns.

Our island bed has provided us with a number of opportunities for merchandising and storage as well. Would you expect anything less from me and my team? The shelf-cubby arrangements on either side of the bed afford room for flowers, candles, the necessary alarm clock, as well as books and other personal effects you might want to keep handy at bedside. The shelf at the top of the headboard is large enough to accommodate a number of objects, including our iconic blue-and-white planter. On the other side of the bed we built shelves to store bed linens, towels, and additional pillows, while a runner over the carpet helps define the "hallway" we created. A slender cabinet and antique prints in gold frames complete the picture.

They say that necessity is the mother of invention. But who knew it could lead us to something so elegant? The lesson learned: Dare to find another way of solving a problem and the results can be surprising.

island bed

materials

4-by-8-foot sheets ¾-inch MDF
(Medium Density Fiberboard)

1-by-12-inch pine boards

Cut three 12-by-72-inch pieces for
the 2 sides and back*

Cut four 12-by-12-inch pieces
for the bottom, top, and
2 shelves*

Cut one 12-by-24-inch piece for
the long shelf (nightstand)*

Cut one 12-by-32-inch piece for
the front*

Crown molding

Wood screws

Wood glue

Finishing nails

Table saw

Miter saw

Caulking gun

Power drill and screwdriver

Hammer

Tape measure

Level

Safety glasses

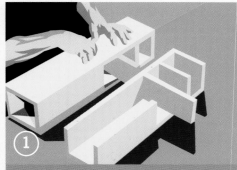

1 Construct a platform from ¾-inch MDF for a queen-size mattress 64 inches wide by 84 inches long by 16 inches high. Install vertical supports underneath the platform spaced about every 12 inches.

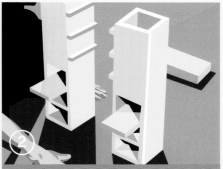

2 Construct a bookcase for the headboard 42 inches high by 64 inches wide by 12 inches deep with 2 shelves and a back.

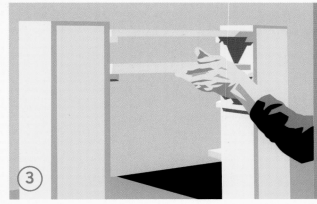

3 Build 2 columns from 1-by-12-inch pine boards 72 inches high by attaching the 2 sides to the back using wood glue and wood screws. Predrill the holes and countersink all screws.

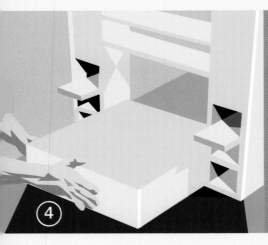

4 Attach 2 bottom shelves to the back and sides of each column, evenly spacing them (approximately 10 inches apart). Attach the long shelf for the nightstand, then another shelf to close the opening in the top of each column. Attach the top to each column, then add the front of each column, screwing it to the side pieces and top. Trim around the top of each column with crown molding mitered at the corners and attached with finishing nails

5 Attach 1 column at each end of the bookcase using long wood screws. Attach the bed platform to the back of the bookcase. Paint or finish as desired.

* Measurements are approximate. Steps shown in miniature.

seaside chic bathroom

YOU KNOW, BATHROOMS can be really tricky when it comes to deciding on a theme, because you have to work with stuff you can't live without and in places you probably wouldn't have chosen for it. On a whim, it would be nice to move the toilet to the other side of the room as if it were a chair, but unfortunately it doesn't work that way. So we have to work with what we find where we find it. In this room we have a couple of sinks side by side, the shower, the toilet, of course, and a whirlpool sort of tub. What do they all have in common? Let's see . . . WATER. Our theme could come from a lake or a river, or even the seaside. Yeah, that's what we'll do, a seaside retreat. It will work great with our bedroom. Now why didn't I think of that? Oh, I just did.

Making your way into the bathroom first thing in the morning can be quite an assault to the senses, so we decided to soften the blow by painting it the same soothing blue as the master bedroom. Recalling an earlier age when the world didn't spin at the frantic pace it seems to now, we treated all the trim with a weathered crackle finish in white and tan, reminiscent of seaside summerhouses at the turn of the last century. (See "Layer 1," right,

LAYER 1: PAINT AND ARCHITECTURE
Crackle finish is such an easy technique, and the crackle medium is now available everywhere. You brush on your base coat (the color that will show through the cracks), then let dry. Then top with the clear crackle medium. When dry, top with a final color. The crackle finish does all the rest. We crackle-finished all the moldings first, then installed them against our rich blue walls. When you look into a room with limited cabinet space, look for any opportunity to add stackable shelves or overhead shelves. They make such a big difference.

LAYER 2: INSTALLED FLOORING
Area rugs will turn the simple vinyl floors into background. But remember, that's Layer 4.

LAYER 3: HIGH-TICKET UPHOLSTERY
We ordered a terry-cloth ottoman, which went in the center of this bathroom, but it didn't arrive before the scheduled photography. This space works as is, but the ottoman brought even more function to it.

LAYER 4: ACCENT FABRICS
We did a simple window treatment over the bath tub. Roman shades are great because they lift completely up and away for splashing. If you want to install a false shade, place a miniblind underneath.

LAYER 5: NONUPHOLSTERED SURFACES
We added a crackle-finished dresser outside the tub area. But instead of the ottoman we ordered, you could also add a small round table to be used with a small stool as a vanity.

LAYER 6: ACCESSORIES
Be sure that your accessories match your theme; otherwise, the overall effect can be a hodgepodge. Cluster items of various heights and shapes together for great vignettes.

LAYER 7: PLANTS AND LIGHTING
This is a utilitarian space, but it should also be a place where you treat yourself to a long bath while you pamper yourself. We love candles in the bathroom, because you can put them anywhere and need not worry about the danger of mixing water and electricity. If you replace your ceiling light with track lighting, then you will be able to focus light where you need it without killing the mood.

Paint Ceiling

MAYBE NOT! MOLDING

DIVISION OPEN SHELVING

ELF IT RE ?

ROMAN SHADE ?

PAINT WALLS

SEA SHORE
WEATHERED
WOOD
WHITE
ACCENTS
SPA
SAND : SEA

CRACKLE
FINISH
(WHITE
DISTRESSED)

PAINT

MOLDING ?

for instructions on how to create this finish yourself.)

There wasn't a lot we felt we could do with this space structurally, but we weren't terribly keen on the idea of looking directly into the corner whirlpool tub, either. We noticed a funny little ledge between the tub and the vanity. We weren't quite sure what it was for (it's probably where the whirlpool mechanism resides), so we thought it might be a good idea to follow some of our own advice: When in doubt, build up. And that's what we did with a simple yet effective shelf unit. We picked up a lot of storage with the shelves, and it also gave us an opportunity to add some much-needed architecture to the room. We now have an excellent area to merchandise. More important, it's a great place to put bath salts and all those things that you don't want to get wet when you're in the tub so you don't have to step out to reach them.

We trimmed out the mirrors with carved wood frames, then applied narrow strips of molding with silicone to create a frame within a frame that gives the mirrors a beveled look. Since the mirrors weren't really joined together, we added a four-tier column of shelving between them. It's a great storage idea that really looks terrific and allows light and air to circulate. And it gave us another opportunity to do more of the crackle finish.

To break up the large focal-point wall next to the shower, we created a 3-D still life, starting with an urn on top of a tall, narrow cabinet, which afforded a surprising amount of additional storage, and wall sconces with candles on each side. A few ferns, sprays of orchids, and decorative wall plaques on the windows complete this inviting makeover.

Here, the dream unfolded as we solved challenges as they arose, but once the dream emerged, it came to life in the act of doing. As you systematically work through the challenges, remember to be flexible and persistent, until you turn that exciting corner where it all comes together! What at first seemed an impossible task turned into one of the most dramatic rooms in the house. In the final analysis, were we able to make this bathroom seaside chic? Will she really be able to sell seashells down by the seashore? You bet your hip waders.

PRECEDING PAGES: The adjoining bath became seaside chic with a deep blue wall color accented with weathered crackle-finished woodwork in white and tan. There was a funny little ledge between the whirlpool tub and the vanity. At first we weren't quite sure what it was for. So when in doubt, build up. That's what we did with a shelf unit.

Unifying Spaces

THE KEY to creating unified master suites, whether large or small, is establishing a clear relationship between the bedroom and the bathroom. In en suite bathrooms we often think we can just close the door so they don't need the same attention. Not really so. The door to the bath is usually open more than it's closed. The first and easiest way to begin the relationship is with color.

The light green tracery we created in the Modern master bedroom was carried through to the bath in the green-stained bamboo trim that replaced the etched-glass divider. The organic textural feeling connects the two rooms, allowing light in. The bold green and cinnabar colors carried into the back shower and tub area keep the continuity of the Zen-sational feeling of the bedroom and incorporate the same bedroom wall colors into the bath.

Organic accessories like wicker baskets hold bathroom necessities, still in keeping with the bedroom theme. The same architectural elements, such as plaques on the wall in both areas and the shower curtain color, which relates to the drapery and bedcovers in the bedroom, further unite the spaces into a single pampering spalike retreat.

For variety, try reversing wall and ceiling colors used in the master bedroom when bringing them into the bathroom. What a completely different yet unifying look you get by cross-pollinating color. Next, pull architectural elements from the bedroom into the bath. Window cornices, columns, and molding all work to unify the two spaces. Finally, choose accessories that further carry the theme through both rooms.

9-by-10 bantam bedrooms

contemporary unisex
built up, not out

WILL YOUR GUESTS FEEL imprisoned if you stick them in a 9-by-10-foot room? That was our next dilemma: creating multifunctional grace in what were really no more than three glorified closets. Well, you've heard me say it so many times, "If you can't build out, build up." But did you know that by build-

ing wall to wall, you can pick up very valuable inches here and there that can help you really stretch space?

In the first tiny back space, our goal was to create a guest room with a decidedly tailored approach. We wanted to make it classic in style, but with a Modern twist: kind of tone-on-tone with a touch of contemporary Zen attitude. We envisioned a decidedly guy-friendly space, like a stateroom on a yacht, in which everything that isn't needed gets thrown overboard. So we chose to build in everything wall to wall. And we're stretching, and we're stretching! Lift those glue guns, people!

Here again, we took a page from the classical Japanese design book and kept all the built-ins low to the ground. Not only is it more compact, but you have a sense of uninterrupted space overhead. A console starts on one side of the room and goes all the way around the wall under the window, where it widens out to a twin-size mattress platform with a ledge on each end, all of it anchored directly to the walls. The supports underneath create a series of intersecting lines to replicate a Modernist graphic effect, much like that found in the paintings of Mondrian. We have centered

THE SEVEN LAYERS

LAYER 1: PAINT AND ARCHITECTURE
To keep the attitude tailored, we chose a monochromatic color scheme ranging from cream to chocolate. We painted first because the openings in our built-in would show the wall color. The wall-to-wall built-ins added multifunction to what seemed a useless room. Once in they, too, were painted, thus completing the shell of the room.

LAYER 2: INSTALLED FLOORING
Tan wall-to-wall carpet had to be installed first because of the built-ins, but by the time the room was complete very little of it could be seen.

LAYER 3: HIGH-TICKET UPHOLSTERY
We treated the bed in the same monochromatic tone-on-tone approach. Even the ottomans reflected this emphasis on texture rather than print.

LAYER 4: ACCENT FABRICS
We kept these to a minimum. Stacked pillows offered formal texture, and window treatments simply added another layer to our tone-on-tone palette.

LAYER 5: NONUPHOLSTERED SURFACES
All hard surfaces were planned in advance to incorporate a console, a bed platform, and storage and table functions. Amazing!

LAYER 6: ACCESSORIES
With an eye to the Asian art of placement, nothing superfluous went into this room. Keeping the accessories to a minimum, we also reduced clutter to create a tranquil mood. Architectural plaques and vertical mirrors stretched the room into new proportions.

LAYER 7: PLANTS AND LIGHTING
Rice-paper shades and symmetrical wall sconces really brought this room into a Zen mood. Candlelight added a spiritual feeling to these great multiuse spaces. There was even enough room for a bonsai tree to underscore the Asian ambience.

Pamper Your Guests

WITH SPACE at a premium, most houses have rooms that need to pull double duty. By keeping rooms multifunctional, you can give guests a place to feel at home and yet be able to use the living space yourself when guests aren't present.

Guests need to have someplace to put all their "stuff" after they've unpacked. The built-in shelving around our unisex guest room provided that space. If your guest room also serves as an office, leave a shelf or two in the bookcase empty so that guests can have a little space to call their own. While you're at it, don't toss those paperbacks just because you're through with them. Maintain a library of the books you really liked for your guests to enjoy. There is nothing like catching up on one's reading while on the road.

It's always nice to furnish guests with a little mirror, some vanity items, and fluffy towels. A few scented candles and plants add a wonderful warmth to the room. Now they can easily get out of bed and prepare themselves for the day with their vanity items.

Ideally, you want your guests to be able to fall asleep as easily as they do at home in their own beds. A lot of high-end hotels are just now figuring this out. (Why has it taken them so long?) They are beginning to equip rooms with a lot of sleep-inducing amenities that would be terrific for us to treat our guests to in our own homes. Thoughtful perks include white-noise machines, which are now quite inexpensive and very effective; sleep handbooks full of suggestions on how to bring on Mr. Sandman; and a stash of hypoallergenic pillows, eye masks, and disposable earplugs.

Another idea is to make up a basket full of the pampering goodies that guests might want to use to make them feel like they're really on vacation. Include some power bars, cookies, candies, bottled water, eyedrops, reading material, and maps of the local area to help them plan their time in your neck of the woods.

Make your guests feel special, but be careful. They may get used to it and never want to leave!

the entire room around the tiny lone window, giving it the strength of symmetry. (See pages 86–87 for instructions on how to build your own unisex guest room.)

If most travelers are like me, and I think they are, it's amazing how much of their belongings they can stuff into a suitcase or two. Yet when I'm ushered by my hosts to what will be my living quarters for the weekend or a few days, I open up my luggage and quickly run out of room to put things. We kept that in mind when we began planning our unisex guest room. Since our space had to function in a number of different ways, we had to make sure there was also room to put away linens, pillows, and extra blankets during the day and swap them out for those things that were required for the room to operate as more of a sitting room–cum–office. That's why one of our first priorities in designing this room— as well as all our other guest bedrooms—was to include as much space for storage as possible. To that end, we provided unifying cubbyholes on each side of an open center, which buys us a ton of storage space. It gets the bed up off the floor and doubles as a settee by day. A double thickness of our favorite building material, MDF (Medium Density Fiberboard), or plywood was used for everything, to provide not only strength but also a Modern line.

The best guest rooms provide plenty of multitasking space. There are phone calls to make, letters to write, day trips to plan, return-home itineraries to put together. With that in mind, we added a small writing desk with an extra stationery shelf and more cubbyhole storage incorporated into the built-in unit on the other wall adjacent to the bed.

All the cubbyhole shelf combinations are painted to match the wall's lush, rich color. The tone-on-tone monochromatic palette makes them feel not only very built-in but also quite substantial.

It was then time for the really fun part. The bed is dressed in a simple pattern, Geosheen, and three pillows are placed very stoically in a single line, because the whole attitude of this room is about symmetry and geometry. It's a very modern look, and again, the key is not too much adornment. Keep it simple. Keep it chic. Keep it unisex. Remember, if you keep it tailored enough for him, yet luxurious enough for her, there's no way to go wrong. Architecture has been added all around the room by applying wide vertical wood panels directly to the walls that go right to the ceiling and painting them a lovely deep chocolate brown. These panels also became the mounting blocks for wall sconces that, along with the luminary columns and the hanging lantern overhead—all softly shaded with that wonderful

"To maximize every inch, build wall to wall."

OPPOSITE: **To stretch the dimensions of the room, long vertical mirror panels were added between the wood panels on opposite walls. This doubles the size of the room and, more important, doubles all the beauty that is in the room.**

unisex guest room

materials

4-by-8-foot sheets ¾-inch MDF
(Medium Density Fiberboard)
or plywood*

Wood screws

Wood glue

Finishing nails

Table saw

Band saw

Power drill and screwdriver

Hammer

Tape measure, pencil, and paper

Level

Safety glasses

Sandpaper

Primer and brush

Paint and paintbrushes

Purchased twin-size mattress

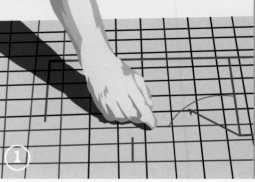

Draw a diagram of the layout of the built-ins with accurate measurements. The width of the bed/seating platform needs to be 3 inches wider than the width of a twin-size mattress. The height should be comfortable for seating, keeping the depth of the mattress in mind.

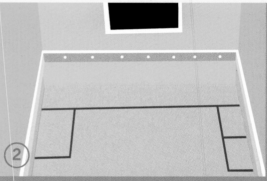

The support structure under the bed consists of 2 shelving units, each of which consists of a horizontal shelf and 2 vertical struts. The shelf is half the width and approximately one-third the length of the bed platform. The upright supports are cut the width of the bed platform by the desired height. Cut two 1½-inch slits in the front edge of the shelf, halfway through the shelf and a quarter of the way in from each side. Cut a 1½-inch slit in one end of each of the 2 upright supports the same length as the slits in the shelf. Slide the slits in the shelf into the slits in the upright supports and secure together with wood glue and screws. Construct a second support structure.

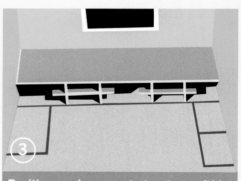

Position each support structure within the wall space and secure to the floor and wall. Cover the supports with the bed platform.

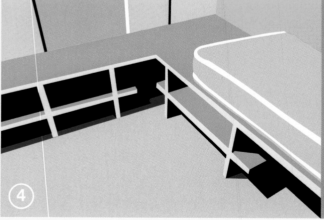

Construct the side wall supports in the same way as the underbed supports. Side wall units use narrower measurements than the bed platform. Secure the side units to the wall and floor and add the top surfaces.

OPPOSITE: All the cubbyhole shelf combinations are painted to match the wall color. The tone-on-tone monochromatic palette makes them feel not only very built-in but also quite substantial.

*Note: All wood pieces are double thickness of MDF.

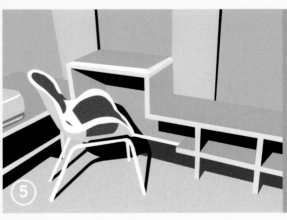

For the desk unit, add a three-sided box to one side unit. One end of the box will rest on top of the bed platform. Secure the 2 units together.

⑤

Sand, prime, and paint as desired. Put the purchased mattress on the bed platform.

⑥

rice paper we love so much—extend the Zen feel all the way around the room.

Wood panels with matching sconces also flank both sides of the window to give the impression that the window is just a little bit bigger than it actually is. The Roman shade reinforces the room's horizontal elements, while the two square off-white architectural panels above the window, as well as the wonderful curtains, make the wall a symphony of texture on texture. And about those curtains: You would never know it to look at the room now, but there is nothing but wall behind them. We even have room for an entire tree in here. Sure, it's a bonsai, but it does a sensational job of bringing the feel of nature indoors—a good idea in any space, essential in a tiny one.

Do you believe all this squeezed into such a little space? You might want to check out that "before" photo again. The best way to decorate a box is to step out of it.

To stretch the dimensions of the room, long vertical mirror panels were added between the wood panels on opposite walls, secured in place by simple clips. Easy. This effectively doubles the size of the room and, more important, doubles all the beauty that is in the room.

Early on in the design process we toyed with the idea of including a chair. We moved around a small task chair we liked for a while during construction. But it never really worked, so instead we decided to push two ottomans together in front of the bed, where they could be used as a coffee table or additional seating during the day. And the nice thing about this arrangement is that one can be easily moved over to the desk area to sit on while writing a letter, when it isn't being used to prop up weary feet. We thought the look was more interesting, and it gave us seating for yet another person. I know. Amazing!

So, we have taken a postage-stamp-size room and created a stateroom with more storage and utilitarian space than many big master bedrooms. You now have great form as well as great functionality in a space that proves you don't have to be afraid of dark color when it's layered properly. During the daytime it's a fabulous sitting area, which will easily accommodate as many as four people, where the bed becomes an upholstered piece. And in the evening, when it's made up, it's the perfect guest bedroom.

RIGHT: Our monochromatic symphony creates an extraordinary space, with function and design, all in a very tiny room. Ship ahoy!

louis, louis:
mail-order french

INSPIRATION FOR THE NEXT 9-by-10-foot bedroom we were presented with came from a makeover we did on the show a few years ago: a little girl's fantasy bedroom with a pair of twin princess beds and cornices. We took that germ of an idea up a great big notch for this small but beautiful French-inspired room. What we've done here probably begs the question: How much molding is too much? By the time we finished tricking out this baby . . . well, you can judge for yourself.

The tendency in small spaces is to stay light with paint color, the theory being that dark colors advance and light ones recede. But just to prove it ain't necessarily so, we painted the room in a deep, dramatic dusty blue. Remember: It's only Layer 1. By the time you get those six other layers done, how much of that color are ya really gonna see anyway? But, more important, we wanted to go over the top with molding to really sell our European French theme. As a stunning contrast against this color, we added white architectural embellishments for a Wedgwood effect. So, again, how much molding is too much molding? Um, well, as far as I'm concerned . . . just go for it!

Okay, look up, Louise. Look at what we created. The fabulous cornice pieces above each window were made with a mail-order product called lincrusta, which is actually a linoleum product that simulates meticulously detailed plasterwork. (See page 96–97 for building instructions.) It

THE SEVEN LAYERS

LAYER 1: PAINT AND ARCHITECTURE
Because our abundance of architectural embellishments would be light in color, we went dark with the walls so the cornice and other molding would pop once installed. The simulated plaster-work turned a nothing room into a French masterpiece.

LAYER 2: INSTALLED FLOORING
Wall-to-wall carpet was installed after all molding and painting were finished. We knew our trim would be cream, so we matched the carpet to it. An accent rug would be added later, in Layer 4.

LAYER 3: HIGH-TICKET UPHOLSTERY
French-inspired side chairs helped play up our European theme. We consider these part of this layer, since the upholstery is complicated. The bed linens were done in an icy sheen, ready to receive the accent fabrics.

LAYER 4: ACCENT FABRICS
The bed hangings mirrored the adjacent window treatment with the two complementary fabric panels. Accent pillows added a feminine touch to this extravagantly dressed sleigh bed. The blue trimmed area rug brought that theme underfoot.

LAYER 5: NONUPHOLSTERED SURFACES
The charming side table and the curio cabinet table were just the right scale to add function to the room without taking up too much footprint.

LAYER 6: ACCESSORIES
With the spotlight on the architecture, we didn't overaccessorize. A few porcelain and silver pieces with a European attitude were all that was needed. In rooms like these, follow the theme. Objects that don't go along will stick out.

LAYER 7: PLANTS AND LIGHTING
An ornate task lamp and a great chandelier added decorative and task light to this fabulous room. With the flicker of candlelight, you are instantly transported back to a historic age. A floral topiary adds a touch of elegance to our Louis, Louis room.

Wall Color Is Background— Be Bold

WHEN choosing wall color, always bear in mind that in the final analysis it will serve primarily as background. Paint is Layer 1 for a reason. Unless you plan on living the life of a Tibetan monk, you are going to be covering up major chunks of wall space with art, lighting fixtures, furniture, architectural embellishments, and so on. For that reason, you can really go much bolder in color selection than you probably think you can. Most galleries and museums paint their spaces stark white, they will tell you, because they don't want anything to detract or distract from the artwork on the walls. My polite response is, "Oh, get over it!" Fact is, lately fine-art spaces have begun experimenting with a wide variety of colors that yield spectacular results. So if these often-staid institutions can loosen up aesthetically, we certainly can also. A great house can run the gamut from subtle understatement to outrageous drama, and having a wide spectrum of wall colors to choose from is absolutely essential in developing a dynamic range.

RIGHT: Coming from each cornice are two curtain panels in coordinating damask fabrics, blue and gold on the outside and pale yellow on the inside. The fabric panels cascade casually over the foot and headboard of the twin-size sleigh bed, creating an elegant statement. Could you just die? The curtains on the window are tied back with great-looking tassels. It's a slightly different treatment, but the two work beautifully together.

"Small furniture in a small space makes the room look even smaller. Size does matter!"

was simply mounted onto pieces of bowed luan (a flexible plywood that we use for a lot of things). The lincrusta frieze molding continues all around the entire perimeter of the room. Since the room had textured walls, we backed the lincrusta with luan so that all the panels were rigid, then screwed them to the wall. It looks like we brought in a whole team of French plasterers, but all our molding and simulated plasterwork was ordered over the phone. It's takeout for designers! How cool is that? To substantiate the walls below the lincrusta, we applied molding panels. We painted them to accentuate the white against the blue and placed classical framed prints inside each one. At one point, early in the design process, we thought about adding a fireplace to the room. But when we got started with all the molding, we decided instead to just keep on going with it. The fireplace would have had to be false, of course, and it would have taken up a lot of wall space, thus limiting our furnishing options.

Not only did we have lots of fun with molding, but we saw an opportunity to show how terrific accent fabrics can really theme a room. Coming from each cornice are two sumptuous curtain panels in coordinating damask fabrics, a blue-and-gold pattern on the outside and pale yellow on the inside. From the cornice on the right the fabric panels cascade casually over the foot and headboard of the twin-size sleigh bed, creating an elegant statement. Could you just die? The

LEFT: All this together, the blue and white with a little lemon yellow, has taken this very innocent little back room and turned it into a sensational tour of Versailles.

lincrusta arch

One 4-by-8-foot sheet ¾-inch MDF
(Medium Density Fiberboard)

One 4-by-8-foot sheet ½-inch MDF
(Medium Density Fiberboard)

1-by-2-inch pine boards

"Wiggle board" or ¼-inch flexible luan

Lincrusta of desired width and design

Wood screws

Lincrusta adhesive

Power drill and screwdriver

Scroll saw

2 compasses secured to a length of
1-by-1-inch pine

Straightedge and pencil

Paintbrush and wallpaper brush

Drapery fabric

Staple gun and staples

Closet dowel and 2 closet pole cups
(optional)

Tape measure

Level

Safety glasses

① Measure the width of the window, which will determine the width of the arch. With a straightedge and pencil, mark the base line of the window width measurement onto a sheet of ¾-inch MDF.

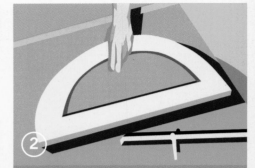

② Place the point of 1 compass secured to a length of 1-by-1-inch pine in the center of the line. Attach the second compass to the end of the pine board 15 inches from the first compass. Swing the pine board, marking an arch on the MDF. Relocate the second compass to a point 12 inches from the first compass and mark the inside arch. Cut out 2 identical arches using a scroll saw.

③ Measure the depth of the lincrusta and cut 8 pieces of 1-by-2-inch pine the length of the lincrusta depth minus 1½ inches (or the thickness of the MDF). Divide the perimeter of each arch into 8 equal sections and mark each section.

④ Secure the pine pieces between the two arches at the marks using wood screws. Predrill holes and countersink the screws. Cut a piece of ½-inch MDF for the back and screw in place.

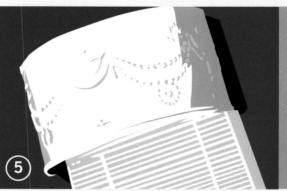

⑤ Cut a piece of wiggle board the circumference of the arch by the depth of the lincrusta. Attach the wiggle board to the arch. Cut the lincrusta to fit the wiggle board.

6 Mark the center point of the arch and the lincrusta. Apply lincrusta adhesive to both the wiggle board and the back of the lincrusta using a paintbrush. Allow to dry until tacky. Place the center marks together, and press the lincrusta onto the cornice. Smooth with a wallpaper brush.

During

7 Paint or finish the lincrusta as desired. To add drapes, either staple fabric to the inside of the cornice, or add a closet dowel and 2 closet pole cups. Stitch a pocket in the top of the drapery fabric and hang from the closet dowel.

curtains on the window are tied back with great-looking tassels. It's a slightly different treatment, but the two work beautifully together, don't you think?

To keep the same brocade feeling down on the bed, we used a neutral, very icy tone-on-tone combination for the bed ensemble. The damask has a cool touch that helps sustain the idea of the plaster influences in the molding all around the room. Cozy, classy, chic. A collection of pillows, all done with moss fringe and rope trimmings, adds just that little French touch this room needs. Well, maybe it had enough "French" already, but we couldn't restrain ourselves. Nor did we have to.

We're not finished with fabrics yet, though. A beautiful area rug was placed on top of the existing wall-to-wall carpet. "Wait a minute," you say, "an area rug is an accent fabric?" That's right. It may be a bit heavier and you walk on it, but it's also part of Layer 4. The blue border of the rug helps bring the color of the walls down underfoot, which we like a lot. Next to the bed sits a fabulous little French curio cabinet that is in scale with the entire room and makes a wonderful still life with a small lamp and mirror.

On the opposite wall, in front of the window, we created another still life with a great little table and two dramatic upholstered side chairs with bolstered pillows. Here again, everything was kept very neutral so it really pops against the blue background. An exquisite corbel with a couple of porcelain figures accents the other wall. Okay, enough already!

All this together, the blue and white with a little lemon yellow distributed here and there, has taken this very innocent little back room and turned it into a sensational tour of Versailles. Very French, don't you think? Hel-lo? Or should I say *bonjour*?

By the way, I understand all the Louis XV this and Louis XVI that can become quite confusing. Not to worry. While there are subtle differences between the two styles, we weren't interested in slavishly sticking to historical accuracy. We needed to know only whether the pieces worked together visually or not. And I think they did . . . handsomely. Of course, if you're interested in finding out more, there are tons of books on classical French furniture and design at your local library. Everybody sing along with me: "Louis, Louis, oh baby now . . ."

bombay with sleigh bed

THE FINAL GUEST BEDROOM is another 9-by-10-foot room, but we thought it would be an ideal place to experiment with lots of dynamic color. While the comforter and bed ensemble (Asian Loom, thank you very much) were the inspiration for this gorgeous, well-traveled British Colonial style, we thought we'd like to try to incorporate some fun things, like monkeys and palm trees as well. Since this room is in the back of the house, we don't have to worry about doing a fantasy room that might otherwise disrupt the visual flow of the rest of the house.

To incorporate the reds and gold of the fabric, the walls were painted a sensational red (Apple Skin). Yes, reds can be a little tricky. We didn't want the room to look like a Red Cross station, but we loved the idea of the Asian Bombay oasis theme. Think Raffles in Singapore on a balmy evening. That's what we were dreaming about.

Remember, paint those ceilings, dear one! We chose a gold paint for the vaulted ceiling, and then we actually brought the color down the wall to create a horizontal edge. A fluted molding was then added over our new false ceiling line to help define where the wall color ends and the ceiling color begins.

For our wainscoting we used anaglypta, an embossed, textured wallpaper product that

THE SEVEN LAYERS

LAYER 1: PAINT AND ARCHITECTURE
Small back rooms can be painted any color you want, as they won't influence the rest of the house. We wanted a red-and-gold theme. We painted first, using molding at the 8-foot line to stop the wall color and introduce the ceiling color, then added a chair rail and wainscoting to begin our world-traveled Bombay theme.

LAYER 2: INSTALLED FLOORING
We kept the cream wall-to-wall carpet, knowing an area rug would cover most of it, but that comes later, in Layer 4.

LAYER 3: HIGH-TICKET UPHOLSTERY
The bed was dressed in a weave-patterned mix of brown, red, and gold—a tapestry feeling that had an Eastern flair. A side chair would add yet another opportunity for upholstery.

LAYER 4: ACCENT FABRICS
At the windows we introduced a basket-weave pattern to coordinate with the grass-cloth wainscoting. Tied-back panels in front of the bed helped define the space and added more fabric to the room, thus changing the acoustics.

LAYER 5: NONUPHOLSTERED SURFACES
We incorporated the side table into our sleigh bed to make it ready for a lamp in Layer 7. The small game table and the armoire created a work and storage surface. Note how much furniture is actually in this small room. The eye goes to the furniture, not to the size of the room.

LAYER 6: ACCESSORIES
With workable surfaces being the point, we kept our artifacts lean. It's a good idea in guest rooms to leave space for your guests rather than filling up all surfaces. But when it came to the birdcage we just couldn't help ourselves.

LAYER 7: PLANTS AND LIGHTING
The handsome lamp on the bed ledge is both useful and decorative. Uplights helped heighten the drama, and a palm tree gave the room that cozy "umbrellaed" feeling.

During

"Use molding to help end one color and start the next."

comes in rolls. For easy installation or textured walls, the anaglypta was pre-mounted onto luan panels with wallpaper paste, then put up all the way around the room and even on the front panels of the bed. (Luan is simply ¼-inch plywood, available in most hardware stores.) The panels were stained gold and the chair rail was capped off with molding carved to give it the appearance of rope. All the trim has been highlighted with gold over a base coat of red, then sanded to give it that old-world texture. So faux-fabulous! Can you stand it?

The big pièce de resistance (and doesn't everybody need at least one of those?) is the bed, which is our own adaptation of a sleigh bed. The mattress sits on top of a plywood box with rails that are scooped down below the window in the back as well as the front. We wedged boxes between the bed and the wall at both ends to give us a ledge on either side that not only adds symmetry but also gives us a place for plants and lamps. We even had plenty of surface on which to place clusters of accessories.

And speaking of the movable objects in the room, if you're not sure where they should go, here's a suggestion that could also be a lot of fun for you to try. Be your own guest. That's right, spend the night in here yourself. You'll quickly discover what works where it is and what doesn't. You can then place the lamps strategically for reading and change the wattage of their bulbs or put them on dimmers. Fine-tune the placement of tables and chairs. Think about those things that would be useful to you if you were visiting from out of town: maps or guide-

LEFT: The bed is painted the same color as the walls, and insets of anaglypta trimmed out with bamboo were added along the front. The gold against the red with that organic touch of bamboo invokes exotic faraway places.

"Upholstery and pillows improve the acoustics and enhance the atmosphere."

books of the local area, a basket with bottled water and aspirin. With this kind of attention to the creature comforts, your guests will never want to leave! So, you better be careful when extending invitations.

The bed is painted the same color as the walls, and insets of anaglypta trimmed out with bamboo were added along the front. Here again, it's the gold against the red with that organic touch of bamboo that invokes exotic faraway places. To tie everything together, we used a fabric similar to that on the comforter and hung curtains on swivel rods on each side of the bed. This created a subtle division between the sleep space and the work space. Let's keep our spaces multitasking, everybody!

For the window treatment we simply took panels of lattice, cut them down, and painted them. These panels interrupt the view (which in our case wasn't all that hot) but allow the natural light to come through, and we like the texture it provides a lot. We added a little birdcage and two fabric panels with a basket-weave pattern. Now that little bitty window has taken on a tremendous presence.

In front of the bed, a rug was placed directly on top of the existing wall-to-wall carpet. On top of that, as the perfect dual-function piece, we placed a great-looking table with a carved pedestal base (no legs at the perimeter to restrict chair placement). It's at the perfect height to act as a bedside table and be treated as a desk when the need to correspond strikes, because during the day the bed will serve as a sofa as well. Two upholstered chairs that match the armoire on the other side of the room were added, so everything is perfectly scaled. Just a little bit of upholstery and the pillows help deaden the acoustics in the room and make it feel more intimate.

Since the closet didn't really serve the room, we took it out and replaced it with an armoire. The armoire is more in keeping with the timeless feel we were going for, while giving us more sumptuous wood texture. Now there's storage space for clothing and, more important, an entertainment center. That way your guests can watch TV in their own room, till all hours if they want, and keep their hands off your clicker, thank you.

Add a few artifacts to help round out the whole scenario and we have taken what was originally a blah little back room and turned it into a separate guest room that will make your guests feel as if they have taken a trip halfway around the world. Be my guest!

OPPOSITE: A few well-chosen artifacts can really define the theme you're working toward.

Large Furniture in Small Rooms

I KNOW it seems like a total contradiction, but the right large pieces will work far more effectively in small spaces than the wrong small ones. The dollhouse effect can be quite alarming, especially when you begin to see people inhabiting your space. This is the perfect time to start thinking outside the constrained box you might have thought of your small home as being. True, you might lose some square footage by going with larger furniture, but simply making up for a lack of volume with underscale pieces will lead to visual disaster. Better a few well-chosen larger things than a bunch of small ones, just so you can say to yourself, "Look at how much stuff I was able to cram into that little bitty room!" Fine, if all you ever invite over are mice.

The scale is especially effective when the large piece is a mirror, because it can double the size of a room with its reflection. Placed opposite a door, with another mirror facing it, a mirror can make a room look like it goes on forever.

But my favorite oversize piece is a big bed. I have been in hotel rooms in Europe so small that they make a 9-by-10-foot room look huge. Often they are outfitted with fully dressed king-size beds that make you feel like you live in a palace. Since the bedroom is for sleeping, and a bed is where you sleep, why not let it take over?

5

two tailored
guest bathrooms
and a
utility room

go plum loco

SO HERE'S THE DEAL when working around built-in color like tile or laminate countertops: If you can't beat 'em, join 'em. Since the folks at Fleetwood Homes gave us a choice of surface colors in two bathrooms, we did one in a natural white. But, with the other one, we decided to bamboozle even ourselves by choosing a scary plum color. It gave us a chance to illustrate for you how to deal with someone else's idea of, um, well . . . aggressive color.

The sink was white, the toilet was white, and the whole tub surround was white. Even the grout between the plum tiles on the sink counter was white. We decided to be kind to ourselves and left all of those elements alone. The background color turned out to be a pretty obvious choice sitting right underneath our noses. So instead of saying, "How do we disguise this color?" we declared, "Let's just do EVERYTHING in plum." The idea here was to AMPLIFY the color.

And that's exactly what we have done. We painted the entire room a dusty plum color, giving us great contrast between the walls and the white trim and white fixtures. We actually wanted the walls to appear a tad warmer than an absolute match of the countertop tiles would have given us. In our experience, as long as the two colors are in the same family and don't stray too far from one another in

OPPOSITE: To scare ourselves, we chose plum-colored tiles for the countertop of a vanity in a small guest bathroom.

THE SEVEN LAYERS

LAYER 1: PAINT AND ARCHITECTURE
With the tile built in and all the fixtures white, we painted the room a dusty plum to match the color of the tiles. If you can't beat 'em, join 'em. After the walls were painted, we added cubbies for architecture and storage. They were built and painted white off-site, then mounted with wood strips. To resolve the mirror, we did a double framing in wood painted white. Liquid nails secure the frame to the glass.

LAYER 2: INSTALLED FLOORING
The choice was simple: It was built in. Later, terry-cloth rugs would be scattered over the white tile.

LAYER 3: HIGH-TICKET UPHOLSTERY
There was no room for upholstery, but in Layer 6 the towels and shower curtain will give an impression of upholstery. A small ottoman is ideal in bathrooms with more space. The human form needs only 18 inches to be mobile.

LAYER 4: ACCENT FABRICS
The shower curtain and towels were a great way to introduce accent fabric. But remember, in small spaces, a lot of pattern could overwhelm the space. When using extreme color, as we did here, limit the number of your accent colors.

LAYER 5: NONUPHOLSTERED SURFACES
Usually the counter would be considered in this layer, but because it is built into the shell of the room, it remains in Layer 1. However, you can see how narrow your options are when you build in specific color.

LAYER 6: ACCESSORIES
Great containers help you store and organize your bath items. We merchandised our cubbies this way, but you can think also of stainless-steel bins or wire baskets. The mirror, now adorned, looks more like an accessory than a built-in, which is good.

LAYER 7: PLANTS AND LIGHTING
I love taking down overhead lights and replacing them with track lighting. That way, you have light that can be focused where you need it and still preserve the room's intimacy. Remember, plants love moisture, and they make you feel connected to nature. An orchid did the trick here, without taking up room.

intensity, the brain will read them as a match. Now the eye bounces from the plum-colored walls to the white sink to the plum tiles on the white vanity to the white commode, then back to plum against the wall, to white around the tub. I know it's a lot of plum . . . but wait: There's more news when the paint dries.

Next, we took nine standard-size five-sided boxes and painted them white. We surrounded the tiny window with these cubbyholes, making it appear three times as big as it actually is. This sleight of hand is an important technique because few things will make a small space feel smaller than badly proportioned windows. In fact, most of the windows in both our Modern and Traditional houses had been, for reasons of cost containment as well as temperature control, smaller than we would have liked. But, fortunately, there are many ways to not only achieve this effect but also keep the results from getting stale. The trick is to apply the technique and still let as much light in as possible, which I think we accomplished.

Very inexpensively, we used white as our theme, created great storage, and also added architecture to the room. Again, white against the plum color—so retro, but with a modern graphic flair. Sort of "back to the future," don't you think? We loved it so much we kept on going. On the opposite wall we added four more boxes. Symmetry is key, and each one of these cubbyholes can be used for him or her, another member of the family, or even a guest. We then carried the white all the way back into the tub area with a white terrycloth shower curtain. Burgundy towels hung over the shower curtain layered the color on top of the white and also added texture. Terrific.

We had a not-so-hot mirror that was attached with only a couple of mirror clips, so we decided to amplify that, too. I love the idea of hanging mirrors on top of mirrors. It gives a really great dimensional look. We framed out the area with pine painted white, then simply suspended an inset mirror, which was also done in pine framing and bead board, from two wires. It really helps play up the plum tile and brings the mirror into scale with the vanity. The mirror is positioned at almost the same height as the boxes, so the eye goes from the white and the plum right in front of you to the white and the plum all the way around the room. An orchid spray lent a touch of organic softness without taking up much space. These kinds of touches make a house your home . . . and reflect your personal creativity.

Take chances with bold color and experiment, because you don't have to worry that what you do in a guest bathroom will interrupt the visual flow of the rest of your home. You can be daring; you can have fun. Plum and white. Works for me.

"Don't be scared, it's only color. Don't panic, paint it!"

OPPOSITE: This bathroom clearly demonstrates that when you have a dominant color built into your room, the rule of thumb is "If you can't beat 'em, join 'em." We surrounded the tiny window with these cubbyholes, making it appear three times as big as it actually is.

a celadon fantasy

NOT EVERY ROOM can go for broke. Here we played it safe with an eye on the resale of the home by choosing a tri-tone green laminate countertop on the vanity with a pickled light undercabinet. That's the good news. The bad news is IT'S AS BORING AS AN OLD WHITE GYM SOCK!

But in this Modern guest bathroom, the redo was all about accessories and color. It was neutral enough that we could bring in aquatic background colors and introduce silver and white accents. We painted the background wall color a Pacific Ocean blue green (Melon Rind) that went well with the sink surround, with a slightly lighter transitional ceiling color. It's not easy being green, unless it's the right shade, of course.

Because of where it is situated in the house, this was the bathroom that would most likely be used by guests during social gatherings. (The house had no powder room.) It was therefore important that it look as good as the public areas of the house. The footprint in the room was so small that we didn't want to interrupt any of the floor space by adding cabinets or furniture. So the walls needed to draw the eye upward, and thereby make the space feel warm and welcoming. More important, because the room was so small, we were looking for items that weren't just decorative, but functional as well. When you have got enough on your

OPPOSITE: We chose a tri-tone green laminate countertop on the vanity with a pickled light undercabinet.

THE SEVEN LAYERS

LAYER 1: PAINT AND ARCHITECTURE
Two shades of green together create an aquatic feeling. It's fresh and clean. The architecture is added to the wall with our silver-painted modular unit. We have actually done this elsewhere floor to ceiling, and it yields amazing storage space.

LAYER 2: INSTALLED FLOORING
Our tile was white and safe. A throw rug will help add softness underfoot.

LAYER 3: HIGH-TICKET UPHOLSTERY
There's was no room for upholstery in this small bathroom. However, a simple terry-cloth toilet-seat cover will give your loo the feeling of an upholstered tuffet.

LAYER 4: ACCENT FABRICS
Your towels and shower curtains will give you plenty of room to introduce accent fabrics. I still recommend using only solids or borders in a room this small. Florals and other strong patterns can be overwhelming.

LAYER 5: NONUPHOLSTERED SURFACES
Our modular wall piece provides storage and looks great. Because it was added to the room rather than built in, it stays in this layer. Even the shelves in the tub area work in this layer and in Layer 1 as architecture.

LAYER 6: ACCESSORIES
Here is where you can have fun with all those great bath containers and accessories and, yes, wall art. Remember, even rolled towels or neatly folded stacks of them can go from being accent fabric to being accessories. Pick a theme when mixing accessories in a small room. We used chrome and white.

LAYER 7: PLANTS AND LIGHTING
We didn't do plants here, opting for a super-streamlined look. But track lighting and candles really played well against our rich-colored walls.

Color and Storage

AS YOU have read, when it comes to intense color, our motto is: If you can't beat 'em, join 'em. In our plum guest bath, we didn't try to disguise the deep tile color; instead, we played it up by painting the walls just about the same color. The white accents pulled the eye around the room and created a jumping-off point to add even more white accents and a lot of storage.

The plywood cubbies we built and painted white supplied architecture for a bland room and much-needed storage. And their placement around the small bathroom window kept frequently used toiletry items within easy reach of the sink, while beefing up the window size substantially.

If you are feeling "constructionally challenged, organizing stores sell a variety of containers—even if they are just simple four-sided boxes with backs—that can easily be painted and hung on the wall. You can attach clusters of wastebaskets or metal buckets to the wall for storing towels and tissue rolls. Be innovative.

We designed a storage unit that also added architecture for our celadon guest bath by stacking purchased cabinets in a cantilevered arrangement. All those bathroom "unmentionables" can now be hidden away. The silvery metallic paint we used on the fronts of the cabinets picks up the silver in the chrome containers and acts as the "jewelry" of the room, pulling the eye to these accents.

For other toiletries, we chose white containers, yet another accent color against the deep green walls.

mind with a turkey in the oven, you don't want to have to keep running back here to see if you have run out of toilet paper or Kleenex. So it's a good idea to have plenty more stocked in places where people are most likely to find them. This concept is key when designing virtually any small space.

We started considering storage articles that would also add architecture to the room and came up with a really great modular arrangement on the wall over the commode. The profile was kept fairly low to prevent the structure from intruding into the small space. We painted two cabinets with pull-down doors, then stacked them on top of a three-drawer unit in a stair-step fashion to give the arrangement more depth and keep it from looking too blocky. We bolted the cabinets together, then attached them to the wall with butterfly clips. This produced plenty of little cubbies for storing the mundane bathroom necessities and unattractive small containers.

Just for architectural interest—to give an elongated design to the stair-steps—we attached three pieces of wood vertically to the unit. These elements took our store-bought storage cabinets and made them look intentional, sculptural, and built-in. Because chrome was going to be the jewelry of the room, we painted all of the front surfaces with silver Hammerite to coordinate with our cool chrome storage containers.

In front of the tub surround, we suspended a silvery shower curtain from a chrome tension rod. Up above, at each end of the shower, open shelf storage secured to the wall held containers, great for displaying bath salts and for keeping everything within easy reach when you're all wet. On the ledges above there are even more chrome-and-white containers. We have even used the tiny horizontal window sill for a loofah sponge, a clock, and a bit of merchandising. Very cool.

Don't forget about wall art in spaces like this, too. One simple print, visible in the mirror, with a modern aquatic theme looks fabulous. Beneath, a chrome towel rack that rests flat against the wall swivels outward so that towels are at arm's reach from the shower. A silver magazine rack hung on the wall holds necessary reading material.

Around the surround, we added some candles and used the back ledge to add another chrome base with a series of candles. Nothing beats having wonderful candles and aromatherapy treats for your guests when

"The smaller it is, the cheaper it is to furnish!"

OPPOSITE: Just for architectural interest—to give an elongated design to the stair-steps—we attached three pieces of wood vertically to the unit. These elements took our store-bought storage cabinets and made them look intentional, sculptural, and built-in. Because chrome was going to be the jewelry of the room, we painted all of the front surfaces with silver Hammerite to match our cool chrome storage containers.

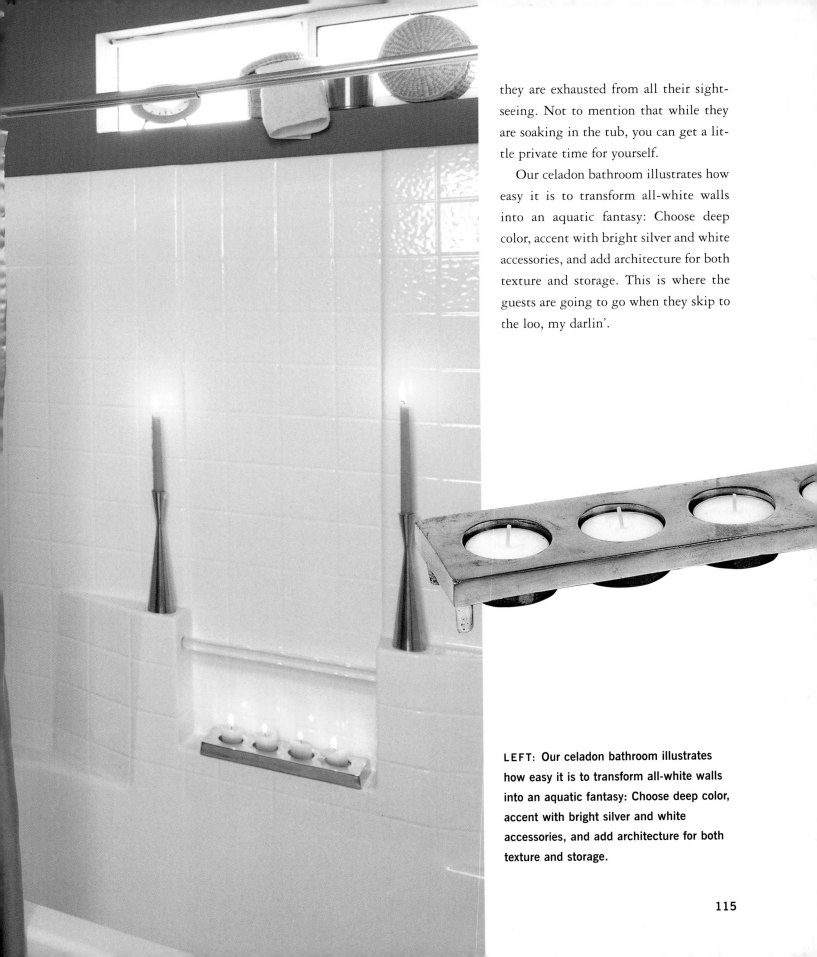

they are exhausted from all their sightseeing. Not to mention that while they are soaking in the tub, you can get a little private time for yourself.

Our celadon bathroom illustrates how easy it is to transform all-white walls into an aquatic fantasy: Choose deep color, accent with bright silver and white accessories, and add architecture for both texture and storage. This is where the guests are going to go when they skip to the loo, my darlin'.

LEFT: Our celadon bathroom illustrates how easy it is to transform all-white walls into an aquatic fantasy: Choose deep color, accent with bright silver and white accessories, and add architecture for both texture and storage.

115

think big
and do the wash

REAL ESTATE is very expensive, so every inch has to count. Many people finally get the courage to do something, but they don't have a creative space that can be devoted to working on it. Believe me, no one understands this better than I do.

In this small utility–laundry room, between the built-in floor-to-ceiling storage cabinet and the wall, there was what looked at first like a useless little niche. After overlooking this space a few times, it occurred to us that it might be just large enough to add a ledge at countertop height as a workstation. Brainstorm! Suddenly all sorts of possibilities began jumping out at us. The ledge itself would be large enough to do some gift wrapping or draw up plans. In fact, if you tackled this area first, you could design the rest of the house from right here.

We added a modular structure above by connecting purchased drawer units vertically and horizontally to keep all those terrific crafting supplies you never know where to put. The nice thing about these units is that the drawers actually come all the way out. You can use them anywhere

OPPOSITE: We installed an ironing board that folds up against the wall by the washer to one side of the space.

THE SEVEN LAYERS

LAYER 1: PAINT AND ARCHITECTURE
"We don't paint utilitarian spaces," you say? But why not? You spend more time there than in your living room. We added a workstation to the existing cabinets.

LAYER 2: INSTALLED FLOORING
The vinyl floors keep this space easy to clean, but if you inherit a bad design, you can simply paint over it and add coats of polyurethane for protection against wear and water.

LAYER 3: HIGH-TICKET UPHOLSTERY
Upholstery may not be appropriate in utilitarian spaces; however, an upholstered work chair might add that needed touch and make you feel good, too.

LAYER 4: ACCENT FABRICS
Chances are this is the spot where you'll be making accent fabrics for the rest of your home. Open shelves with stacks of fabric bolts can look very cool.

LAYER 5: NONUPHOLSTERED SURFACES
In this space, we have a workstation and a washer and dryer. Some folks add fold-down surfaces on piano hinges over the tops of these appliances. Neat idea, huh?

LAYER 6: ACCESSORIES
Once again, this is probably the room where you'll make accessories. And when you do, keep a photo record of them to keep those ideas handy and portable. The concept here is organization: everything in its place. Decorative containers to the rescue.

LAYER 7: PLANTS AND LIGHTING
Replace harsh, unflattering overhead lighting with track lighting and halogen bulbs so that you spotlight what you want and leave the rest in the dark. A drafting lamp clamped to your workstation or an overhead shelf can be cozy too.

"Remember, there are no small rooms, only small imaginations."

in the house and simply stick them back in when you're through. So cool. In addition, that floor-to-ceiling cabinet can now be used to stow your art paper, fabric swatches, and a lot of the other materials that facilitate creativity.

A little magazine rack with a lot of personality was installed below the wall structure. You can keep some of your ideas here within easy reach. It works as a stationery holder or a place to put your bills (maybe not the most inspiring function, but necessary nonetheless). It keeps you organized and up to speed. Here, as in the guest bathrooms, we have added storage containers—perfect for all those clever "no-sew" craft ideas you have been wanting to try. A wall-mounted holder keeps the iron in place; we installed an ironing board that folds up against the wall by the washer on the other side of the space. By the way, a lot of folks might say, "It's a laundry room. I don't want to spend any more time in there than absolutely necessary. Why even bother to paint it?" But we know better, don't we? Since this is now the birthplace of a lot of our creative endeavors it is important to make it as nurturing as possible. To that end we painted the walls mauve (Nutmeg and Rose), while the trim got a coat of cheery yellow called Shitake.

We have transformed a seemingly useless space into a place where we can spur on our creativity. And while you are in the middle of writing your first novel, you can get your underwear and socks out of the washer and into the dryer. Who says creativity and practicality can't coexist in the same space? Not me!

OPPOSITE: A little magazine rack was installed below the wall structure. It works as a stationery holder or a place to put your bills to keep you organized and up to speed. We added storage containers—perfect for all those clever "no-sew" craft ideas you have been wanting to try. A wall-mounted holder keeps the iron in place.

one
diminutive
dining room

drapery envelops a formal dinner party

A FORMAL DINING ROOM in a small space? No way! Well, if you use your imagination and lots of texture, having that luxury can actually be within the realm of possibility.

In our Traditional home, the dining area was really just an extension of the living room, with a hallway that led to bedrooms running right through it. A casual pass-through countertop with overhead cabinets separated the kitchen from the dining area. Through that opening, your guests could peer across the dining table and see the remains of your afternoon of dinner preparations in the kitchen. Not a pretty sight. We wanted to find a way to create a solid unit when guests were dining, yet retain the ability to open it up to make use of the pass-through area.

One wall had a sliding glass door in the center with minimal wall space on either side. And the wall opposite the kitchen was just a solid, plain wall. Excuse me, but . . . boring! We liked the wood in the kitchen cabinets, so our first thought for introducing warmth and texture into the space was to cover the walls in birch paneling. We measured everything meticulously, cut openings for plugs and switches, and before we could say, "Dinner is served!" we stood back to admire our handiwork and went . . . "Hate that!" I know it's hard to believe, but the Christopher Lowell team actually makes mistakes, too. Why just the other day . . . um, you don't really need to hear about that.

Anyway, the inspiration for the final formal look of the

THE SEVEN LAYERS

LAYER 1: PAINT AND ARCHITECTURE
We painted the room but felt it needed more. Fabric was the trick to give this space a theatrical look. The metallic-colored velvet added texture. If that's beyond your budget, use white cotton and put uplights behind it: The whole wall will light up. Very Philippe Starck!

LAYER 2: INSTALLED FLOORING
Because this room was part of an open space, we used the same carpet wall to wall. Keep floor surfaces in public spaces as similar to each other as possible; it helps the visual flow.

LAYER 3: HIGH-TICKET UPHOLSTERY
The stunning dining chairs were all the upholstery this room needed. With the velvet-draped walls, any more would be overkill.

LAYER 4: ACCENT FABRICS
The velvet walls acted as both accent and overall wall color. The chair upholstery, although solid, provided such a contrast that it could also be considered an accent fabric. A runner of place mats on the sideboard is another way to add accent fabrics to a dining room. On the floor, the Oriental runner brought pattern and theme underfoot.

LAYER 5: NONUPHOLSTERED SURFACES
The sideboard addressed storage and display. The table was just the right scale, providing space for up to six guests. Because this room is next to the kitchen, it is a great place for kids to do homework—you can keep an eye on them while you prepare dinner. Just make sure the table surface is durable.

LAYER 6: ACCESSORIES
Similar color and style unify the accessories. Because the objects work better as a grouping, they are clustered together rather than scattered here and there individually.

LAYER 7: PLANTS AND LIGHTING
This is a mood room, so lighting should be flattering. Foot dimmers control the two silver floor lamps and the chandelier. Here, candlelight takes the forefront while dining but never provides enough light to see the food, so dimmed lighting is a key addition. The palms with uplights cast dramatic theatrical shadows.

PAINT CEILING

UPGRADE

MATCHING
PEWTER BASE
LAMPS

AREA RUG

BENCH / STORAGE

STORAGE
SIDE BOARD

CROSS
LINKER

"Don't decorate with your ego, do it with your heart."

dining room came from the cross-linking device we built to separate the living room from the dining area. It is basically two plywood boxes with flat surfaces where we could put great big palm trees, joined by an upholstered seat with a storage shelf underneath. (See page 127 for building instructions.) That gave us an amazing focal point in the room and a Hollywood-inspired feeling that crystallized the treatment for the rest of the space. What a cool idea.

That theatrical theme suggested we hang opulent fabric panels from a curving curtain rod that runs around the perimeter of the dining room. The result is that the dining table now acts as a stage for any meal. The curtain rod surrounds the corner of the kitchen cabinets so the drape can be closed to hide the kitchen area or pulled back for serviceability. The velvet drapes all the way down the wall and falls in soft, luscious puddles on the floor. A valance over the top of the sliding glass doors interrupts the overall drape and reveals the outdoor light. Since privacy and excessive sunlight were not issues we had to contend with, the doors were left uncovered. But covering them as well would be an easy and effective option.

To seclude the area from the Traditional living room, we placed two large Kentia palms on top of each platform of the settee. When you walk around the settee, the mystery of the Zen-sational dining room is revealed. Dupioni silk accent pillows on the settee tie the colors of the living room and dining room together.

Along the wall we placed a sideboard with a very contemporary look. A real find, it's made from dark mahogany with a raised glass shelf. A round table, also in rich, dark mahogany, and four chairs were added to the center of the room. The table and sideboard are just the right scale for each other and the room. And there might be just enough space at the table to add a couple more dining chairs if necessary. Of course, a table with removable leaves that stow away would allow room for even more diners. That way you set the limit.

Anchoring the dining table and chairs is a luscious Oriental area rug. Its muted tones define the furniture cluster without upstaging the tranquil atmosphere of the room. All the colors are tone on tone. The upholstery on the dining room chairs is just a couple of tones lighter than the velvet that's all around the room, giving the space a serene monochromatic look.

On both sides flanking the sideboard, we placed contemporary wooden lamps painted in an opulent, yet understated, silver leaf. Black shades direct a limited amount of light down and up, creating interesting mood shadowing at midlevel. The symmetry of the lamps on either side is very calming. The small shades on the multilight chandelier over the table further diffuse the light and add texture. Marvelous!

Accessories on the sideboard and table, mostly in celadon, were kept minimal for an uncluttered look and to leave plenty of room to place serving platters and bowls that would otherwise have to remain on the table or be hustled in and out of the kitchen. Substantial objects adorn the sideboard beneath the glass shelf, making a very deliberate formal statement without getting in the way.

So there you have it, a very simple treatment. Even though our initial instinct for adding warmth to the room with wood paneling didn't yield the intended results, it didn't mean we had to surrender. Feel free to keep working toward a solution until you're happy with it. That's the key. We ended up with a calm, glamorous dining room. We're ready for our close-up, Mr. DeMille.

ABOVE: Accessories on the sideboard and table were kept minimal for an uncluttered look. Large objects adorn the sideboard beneath the glass shelf, making a very deliberate formal statement. The surface of the sideboard was left open to be used as serving space while entertaining.

> "It's not small, it's special. Remember, big things can live in small spaces."

Adding Fabric to Create Warmth

A DINING ROOM without fabric can seem awfully cold. Just think about spending a long romantic evening enveloped in deep, rich colors and flickering candlelight. You want to keep the light pooled where you need it and only as intense as is absolutely necessary. You want your guests to see each other (and you) in soft light against soft backgrounds. Few things can evoke romance better than richly textured fabric.

Even in this small dining room, we created a theatrical Hollywood feeling by draping almost the entire room from floor to ceiling in a rich-colored velvet. To make it easier we found a curtain rod that we positioned close to the ceiling and extended it around the room.

The curved pieces of the rod were made to go around inside or outside corners. When we put up the rod, it extended around the outside of the kitchen cabinets, which allowed us to completely hide the kitchen when the drapes were pulled.

We shirred fabric directly on the rod, but draperies could also be created using purchased panels attached to curtain rings that effortlessly slide onto the rod. It would be easy to cover a sliding glass door if privacy were desired, then push the draperies to one side to offer access to the door. For a formal luncheon, you will probably prefer sunlight streaming in from a window to brighten the room, in which case you can simply swing the curtains away.

To keep guests from wandering off prematurely, we added comfortable seat and back cushions to the chairs. It doesn't matter how good the food is, your guests won't remember your wonderful cooking if they're forced to shift from side to side on hard-seated, stiff-backed chairs.

settee-divider

materials

Three 4-by-8-foot sheets
   ¾-inch MDF (Medium
   Density Fiberboard)
Two 20-inch-long 1-by-1-inch
   wood strips
2 piano hinges (optional)
3-inch-thick upholstery foam
Upholstery fabric
Wood screws
Table saw
Power drill and screwdriver
Sandpaper
Primer and brush
Paint and paintbrushes
Tape measure
Safety glasses

① Using ¾-inch MDF construct 2 boxes 30 inches high by 12 inches wide by 24 inches deep. If you will be using the boxes for storage, hinge the tops with piano hinges and add bottoms. Add a center support at the bottom if desired.

② To support the seat and center shelf, glue and screw two 20-inch-long pieces of 1-by-1-inch wood to each box to form rails 8 inches and 16 inches from the bottom. Position the boxes 30 inches apart with the rails facing inward. Cut two 24-by-30-inch pieces of MDF and attach them to the rails with wood screws.

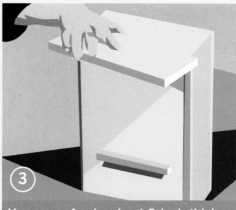

③ Have a professional cut 3-inch-thick upholstery foam 24 inches by 30 inches for the seat cushion. Cover with upholstery fabric.

④ Sand, prime, and paint the settee as you wish. Add the upholstered seat cushion.

⑤ Add a few pillows for the final touch, and VOILÀ.

Steps shown in miniature.

back-tract
kitchens of the future
and a
nondining room

take-in
in a tiny space

IN OUR FIRST KITCHEN, after selecting the most neutral cabinet wood offered, we wanted to introduce more color to keep the space contemporary. So a blanket decision was made to paint all the cabinets. What? Paint wood? I know, guys especially cringe when we even suggest the idea of applying paint to wood that's already been finished, but just because it's wood doesn't mean it's good for the look you're going after. By choosing to paint, we were able to open up so many more options for our design palette. We chose a rich, cheery, creamy butter color in keeping with the attitude of the rest of the adjoining rooms.

A word on the flooring: Sure, it's boring, but it was a perfect background for what we had in mind so we left it alone. But still things were a bit disconnected. The space over the kitchen sink, for instance, seemed totally wasted. So the first thing we did was join the left cabinet to the right, by placing thick modern

OPPOSITE: In our first kitchen, after selecting the most neutral cabinet wood offered, we wanted to introduce more color to keep the space contemporary. We chose a rich, cheery, creamy butter shade. Hip new hardware pieces add a modern effect to the room.

THE SEVEN LAYERS

LAYER 1: PAINT AND ARCHITECTURE
By introducing color to the cabinets, we gave this space a fresh modern update. Connecting shelves are all the architecture needed to put this room in proper balance. Touches of silver paint will come into play later as we begin to introduce chrome and stainless steel.

LAYER 2: INSTALLED FLOORING
This kitchen has typical vinyl flooring, and we left it in place since it was in good shape. For those of you who have bad vinyl floors and little money, paint and polyurethane them. If your vinyl floors are in good shape and relatively flat, try "peel and stick" tiles applied right over the existing flooring.

LAYER 3: HIGH-TICKET UPHOLSTERY
Since upholstery is tricky in areas where food prep and water are a constant, we reserved the upholstery for the other end of the kitchen. More on that later.

LAYER 4: ACCENT FABRICS
We chose not to add fabrics at this end of the kitchen, but they will show up on the other side. People often use "kitchen" motifs such as flowers and foods. Be careful of how you mix these patterns. I prefer simple solid accents in a utilitarian space.

LAYER 5: NONUPHOLSTERED SURFACES
Our shelves will accommodate display items. We removed the pantry door so that it now functions as an open kitchen hutch. We added a center island and began to introduce stainless steel for a modern, yet still warm, feeling. Below, a lower shelf provides even more storage.

LAYER 6: ACCESSORIES
We placed chrome kitchen containers evenly around the room and installed new half-arch oversize drawer pulls to bring the traditional cabinets into the modern age. Here again, less is best in a modern environment.

LAYER 7: PLANTS AND LIGHTING
We replaced the overheads with drop fixtures for a more modern look. Track lighting is ideal to keep light focused where you want it. We will reserve plants for the other side of the room.

ABOVE: We wanted to offset the traditional feeling with a touch of high-tech drama. So when we removed the existing hardware from the cabinets for painting, we replaced them with fabulous contemporary stainless-steel handles. OPPOSITE: The space over the kitchen sink seemed totally wasted, so the first thing we did was join the left cabinet to the right by placing thick modern shelving over the window.

shelving over the existing window. And what a great place it turned out to be to unburden the kitchen cabinets and accessorize with all those neat serving utensils that can decorate a space like this so well. We loved it so much that we did the same treatment over the desk area at the end of the kitchen. (That would soon become our dining area, but more about that in a minute.)

We opened the pantry and loved the idea of removing its door altogether. Why not make this hidden space a focal display area for even more decorative storage? Can't you just see piles of bright-colored plates and great oversize platters and serving pieces tucked neatly in there? The roll-about island, which came with the kitchen, seemed underscale in the space. A larger work surface would work much better for food prep. And if we extended the top just six inches beyond the edge of our new island, we could also make it function as an eat-in breakfast table or even a stand-up bar.

We then wanted to offset the traditional feeling with a touch of high-tech drama. So when we removed the existing hardware from the cabinets for painting, we replaced them with fabulous contemporary stainless-steel handles.

Oh my, how amazing! Stainless steel became our new best friend. It was the icon we were looking for. Remember, when you hit upon an icon, go for it! We

"Even small spaces need room to breathe. If it doesn't function, forget it!"

painted the backs of our newly installed shelves with a paint product called Hammerite. When dry, it looks just like pewter. That helped us begin to spread this new element evenly around the room. To replace the island, we found an inexpensive assemble-yourself wooden table at IKEA. The top was still too small to eat around, so we took our dimensions to our friends at Frigo Design and asked if they could "skin" a larger piece of plywood in real stainless steel that we could put over the existing top. For small change they said, "Why not?" (See Resources, page 168.) We found four wood-and-stainless-steel chairs, whose folding legs allowed them to be easily stored in the pantry where they would be out of the way during food prep.

While we were at Frigo, we remembered that they made kits you could order to alter the appearance of your appliances. So we bought one to reface the dishwasher and another to tone down the dominant refrigerator front. We knew at this point that with a few well-appointed chrome, ceramic, and porcelain accessories, we would be well ahead of the game. Our theme was locked in. For lighting, we found very sleek stainless-steel light fixtures (with frosted shades for a soft effect), which we positioned strategically over the work areas.

We made our Modern kitchen serene and stylish by running the lines of the existing shelving around the perimeter of the space and adding chrome highlights and stainless-steel surfaces for jewelry throughout. High-tech turns out to be ultracool, don't you think? Yeah, me too.

OPPOSITE: We made our Modern kitchen serene and stylish by running the lines of the existing shelving around the perimeter of the space and adding chrome highlights and stainless-steel surfaces throughout. We found an inexpensive assemble-yourself wooden table at IKEA. The top was still too small to eat around, so we took our dimensions to our friends at Frigo Design and asked if they could "skin" a larger piece of plywood in real stainless steel that we could put over the existing top.

demi–dining area

NOW, AT THE OTHER END of the room . . . With no real dining room, we were left with no choice but to squeeze one in next to the existing desk. Desk? you ask. Next to the kitchen? Hmmm. I think the builder's idea was to give you a place to pay bills and write shopping lists, but we put our bills

in the great new utility room (see page 116). Just because they call it a desk doesn't mean we have to treat it as one. We decided that the "desk" would function much better for us as a built-in sideboard.

We brought in a round glass table supported by a simple yet elegant pedestal, and then added upholstered chairs. Adding fabric here gave this end of the space a more formal feeling. But, when in place, the dining set looked a bit cramped. Mirror magic once again to the rescue!

We went to Loose Ends and ordered a roll of grass mat, which we used to upholster an entire wall. Painted wooden slats covered the staples that we used to hang the rugs. The result was divine—just the backdrop we needed against which to lean a huge, gutsy mirror. The mirror's frame matched the

OPPOSITE: We wanted to squeeze in a real dining room next to the existing "desk."

LAYER 1: PAINT AND ARCHITECTURE
We continued our color scheme to the other side of the kitchen. Installing connecting shelves over what will now function as the sideboard provided additional storage, while adding interesting architecture as well.

LAYER 2: INSTALLED FLOORING
The same vinyl floor runs through the whole kitchen, so another area rug will be placed under the new dining room table in Layer 4.

LAYER 3: HIGH-TICKET UPHOLSTERY
We've used our dining chairs to add upholstery to this space. Its clean modern fabric helped play up our clean modern kitchen.

LAYER 4: ACCENT FABRICS
On the wall dividing the kitchen from the laundry room, we affixed imported grass rugs. The organic texture tied in nicely to the area rugs of similar texture. Our natural Roman shade was perfect for the window.

LAYER 5: NONUPHOLSTERED SURFACES
Both the new stainless-steel island and our eat-in table provided valuable function to the room. The built-in counters and sideboard inherited in Layer 1 also contributed greatly to the performance of this space.

LAYER 6: ACCESSORIES
We wanted to make sure that we kept our space clutter-free to make dining easier. To maintain our modern look, we added only a few more chrome pieces. However, the floor mirror made this space stunning and doubled its size.

LAYER 7: PLANTS AND LIGHTING
The bonsai did the trick when it came to the plants. Its architectural shape and scale were controlled and definite. We placed a lamp on the sideboard that added just enough fill light; candles illuminated the table for dining.

Window Shelves

LOOK out your kitchen window. What do you see? A dark and dingy alley? A not-so-pretty apartment building? Your neighbor's garage or, even worse, his garbage cans?

To disguise a less than desirable view yet retain the light, we came up with the idea of building a wall of shelves—glass, wood, or even stainless steel would work—that extended across the expanse of window. It is a treatment that's not only functional but flexible as well.

In our Modern kitchen we wanted to extend the line of the shelves that were already built into a pantry. By removing the door of the pantry we were able to visibly create horizontal lines all around the room. Along the wall above the kitchen sink, we followed the same line of the shelves from the divider and installed shelves all the way to the end of the counter.

We unified the shelving by painting the edges of the installed shelves the same color as the cabinets, but did the shelves' interior with Hammerite. The high-tech silvered look ties into the stainless steel on the kitchen island tabletop as well as the refrigerator.

The window provides a backdrop of colorful glasses, bowls, and other assorted objects on the shelves. By displaying attractive tableware, we kept clutter out of the kitchen and saved room in the cabinets for utilitarian utensils and pantry items. The display is now also visible from the outside, adding a touch of jewelry to the exterior of the house. We think that looks sensational.

"Clutter kills! Don't pack it— pitch it!"

dining room table and gave it a relationship, while its reflection visually doubled the size of the newly appointed dining space and the kitchen beyond.

By adding a few scatter rugs in organic fibers and a few droplights instead of the bare overhead fixture, we went from tract to terrific without breaking the budget. There was even enough room for one of those spectacular bonsais, which we used here as a centerpiece. This space wasn't even a room when we started and now it's transformed into a dining area anyone could be proud of. It's about imagination. It's about paint. It's about accessorizing. That's all it is.

So for next to nothing, you can paint and you can resurface, with the understanding that high-tech means modern now. If you can get up in the morning, get yourself dressed, and put on a few pieces of jewelry, you already know how to do this. If you can dream it, you can do it!

OPPOSITE: We decided that the desk could function much better as a built-in sideboard. We have transformed this space with nothing but paint, accessories, and imagination. ABOVE: Mirror magic to the rescue!

old-world blender

S OMETIMES ONE PERSON'S TRASH can become another person's treasure. We rescued a copper bowl from the side of the road just before the garbage truck scooped it up. A little copper cleaner and some elbow grease transformed what looked like junk to most folks into our old-world kitchen icon. So

keep your eyes peeled and be ready to do some Dumpster diving. You could be rewarded with buried treasure. Bear that in mind as we take you through our Traditional kitchen.

Our second kitchen was the same size as the first but overlooked a dining room on the other side of a pass-through area. (See chapter 6 for more on the dining room.) Since we were going for a traditional old-world feel, we felt the wood finish of the cabinets was appropriate but needed to be beefed up with bigger

LEFT: We rescued this copper bowl from the side of the road just before the garbage truck scooped it up. So keep your eyes peeled—you could be rewarded with buried treasure. OPPOSITE: Our second kitchen was the same size as the first but overlooked a dining room on the other side of a pass-through area.

THE SEVEN LAYERS

LAYER 1: PAINT AND ARCHITECTURE
To give this space more substance we beefed up the kitchen cabinets by adding molding to them. It is always easier to embellish what exists rather than tear out and rebuild. We then painted the space with the two wall colors and the ceiling and trim colors that corresponded with the living room. After the paint dried, we added overhead shelves and the finishing corbels.

LAYER 2: INSTALLED FLOORING
The white textured vinyl floor was what it was; a few scatter rugs would help break it up in Layer 4.

LAYER 3: HIGH-TICKET UPHOLSTERY
We were going to choose an upholstered colonial love seat in a Queen Anne style and chairs, but we chose a Mission-style bench instead to complement our masculine Mission-style table.

LAYER 4: ACCENT FABRICS
We chose the same fabric in two color waves. A formal treatment classed up the window at the end of the kitchen, but a simple café style was all that was needed at the sink. To save money on curtain hardware, try simple-to-use closet doweling and screw-in finials. When painted the same as the walls, they blend in.

LAYER 5: NONUPHOLSTERED SURFACES
Our Mission-style table made from mail-order pedestals matched our benches perfectly. If you hate your tabletop or it's the wrong size or shape, cut a new one out of MDF (Medium Density Fiberboard). Trim it out in molding, then paint or faux-finish it. Apply a few coats of polyurethane and you're in business. Place it directly over the old top. Who knew?

LAYER 6: ACCESSORIES
When you find serving pieces you like, ask yourself if they will go with your kitchen décor or theme. This approach makes display and merchandising much easier.

LAYER 7: PLANTS AND LIGHTING
I hate overlit kitchens; they remind me of cafeterias. Overhead lights are just stock items supplied by most builders. Replace them! Don't be afraid to add uplights, trees, and lamps to these spaces for a warm and inviting feeling. Undercabinet lights are a must for illuminating your work surfaces.

molding to heighten the sense of architecture. We removed the existing 2-inch crown molding from the cabinet tops and replaced it with a 4-inch crown that helped give the cabinets a more custom look.

We found stair spindles, split them lengthwise, and applied them to the cabinets for a carved look. Adding to, rather than tearing out, is the most efficient solution for surfaces that don't measure up. Since the additions increased the scale of the cabinetry, more generous brass hardware was in order as well. While we were at it, we felt there was a lot of wasted space above the cabinets on the opposite wall. From there to the top of the vaulted ceiling we added shelves supported by carved corbels found in a mail-order catalog. This additional overhead display area was perfect for unburdening the cupboards of bulky serving pieces. We loved the corbel idea so much that we also added more of them underneath the upper cabinets to give the appearance that the cabinet unit was one entire hutch. Now that the room's architecture was a bit more substantial, it was time to introduce color.

One of the objectives in doing a kitchen is minimizing the contrast between the cabinets and their surrounding walls. We began by painting the walls with some very rich color combinations. The kitchen ceiling was painted in the same deep sage green (Roasted Celery) used in the living and dining rooms and the hallways. This color wrapped around from the ceiling down the wall to the top of the cabinets. The rest of the wall was painted a soft rust color called Pumpkin

Pie, and an accent wall at the end of the room was painted a deep rust known as Braised Cantaloupe. By surrounding the wood cabinets with a color that is so close to their own, they virtually blend in.

Plates and plants accessorized the overhead shelving, giving the area a lot of presence. Now the room had tons of storage. A great idea to keep in mind when dealing with kitchens is that open storage allows you to show off your beautiful pieces, and reduces the number of objects you have to cram inside the cupboards, thus freeing them up for utilitarian things you would really rather not have to look at.

Fleetwood Homes usually builds an island into the middle of the kitchen in this particular model house, but we asked them to put the island on casters instead. Since so much of what makes a kitchen efficient is the relationship between the various work areas, if the primary prep surface can move closer to the refrigerator to load up with all your ingredients, then roll over to the sink for washing and peeling, then over to the stove to cook, it will save time and a bundle on running shoes.

A small countertop and pass-through space separated the kitchen and formal dining room. To close off the area, we put curtains up all the way around the entire dining room. (See page 124 for further details.) The curtains were beautiful rich velvet on one side and white on the kitchen side to match the countertop. These can open easily for pass-through space or can be closed to maintain the intimacy you want in the dining room when you have guests. More important, when you are entertaining, all your dirty dishes are hidden. We like that a lot.

For even more mood, we placed a warm downlight under the cooktop hood

OPPOSITE, TOP: We upgraded the hardware and added molding between the cabinet doors to give them a more custom look. **OPPOSITE, BOTTOM:** To separate the kitchen and formal dining room, we decided to put curtains up around the entire dining area. **ABOVE:** If you have beautiful serving pieces, put them on display and save the cabinets for the stuff you don't want to see.

"If we are how we live, rise and look around you!"

and accent lights under the cabinets. These make it much easier to see what we're doing when we prepare meals, and they don't break the mood.

The hardware was upgraded slightly, adding a bit of jewelry to the room. Since the appliances we inherited were white, we refaced them with deep chocolate panels from our friends at Frigo that blended perfectly with the wood cabinets. Hanging light fixtures of rice paper with flecks of gold leaf overhead added lots of warmth to the room instead of the straight center light that had been there. Remember, even in a kitchen, lighting is very important and can impart a great deal of mood.

Over in the breakfast nook we started by building a Mission-style table, inspired by legs that were purchased from a mail-order catalog. (See page 147 for building instructions.) The rectangular top, stained to match the wood in the room, provided ample space for four to eat comfortably. We had originally thought of using a Queen Anne–legged love seat and chairs, but the more we looked at our new masculine table the clearer it became that they would be too feminine to make it a true ensemble. Instead, we matched upholstered benches featuring Mission-style arms, and the whole arrangement added a lot of warmth, texture, and a bit of antiquity to the space. What a great find!

Against this rich wall color, we did a wonderful layered window treatment with a false Roman shade. On each side of the window we stitched jabots in the same fabric. Then we added a swag over the top, also in the same fabric, but in a different color—a bold pumpkin. The curtains over the window above the sink were also made from this fabric to tie the two areas together thematically. Below, we hung café curtains, which gave fullness to the mid-level of the room. The window is flanked by a couple of tall topiaries that balance the height of the window treatment and give the area a tremendous amount of substance.

What I love the most about this kind of transformation is how much has been accomplished just with color and by "adding to" instead of completely replacing. These are the creative steps that save a lot of money. Mies van der Rohe may have believed, "God is in the details," but I say "Don't sweat the small stuff." A big kitchen doesn't have to be a daunting proposition. It's just a matter of keeping everything in scale. Throw a bit of upholstery into the mix and watch the whole room come alive.

OPPOSITE: Color, a few accents here and there, and a little bit of upholstery can really make a room come alive.

mission-style table

Cut a piece of ¾-inch plywood the desired size of the tabletop. Measure the distance between the 2 bolts that secure the existing tabletop support to each of the pedestals and make corresponding marks on the plywood. Using a hole maker, drill 1-inch holes in the plywood at the marks. On the underside of the plywood, mark a grid of lines to indicate where screws will secure the plywood to the finish grade pine tabletop. Attach the plywood tabletop onto the 2 pedestals with wood screws from above.

Cut the tabletop from finish-grade pine the same size as the plywood. From below, attach the pine top to the plywood using wood screws spaced every 2 inches along the grid lines to prevent warping. By joining the pieces from below, no screws will be visible on the top.

Cut the table side trim pieces from 1-by-3-inch pine and miter the corners.

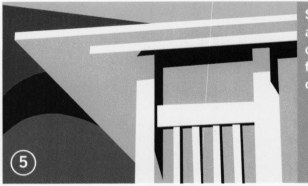

Glue the trim to the edges of the tabletop and secure with finishing nails. Countersink the nails using a nail set and fill with wood putty.

Sand the wood surfaces and stain the table as desired with wood stain followed by several coats of polyurethane.

8

double-duty
public spaces

guest bedroom–den–
family room, anyone?

ONE OF THE CHALLENGES many families face in small homes is there's barely enough living space for themselves, let alone their occasional guests. In cramped quarters, sometimes a second room devoted entirely to guests just isn't a practical option. So some rooms have to serve double or even triple duty. In this case, a small 10-by-10-foot area at the end of a long living room, just beyond the front door, was actually space provided to include some sort of den area. I know this is the kind of small space that could make a person crazy. Some of you are already saying, "I can't do anything with it. Don't even want to try." But if you stop to consider the specifics, you'll realize it's not so scary after all.

With square footage at a premium, it fell to this awkward little space to serve as guest accommodations. Loosely translated, this means, "Grandma sleeps on the couch or gets herself a hotel room!"

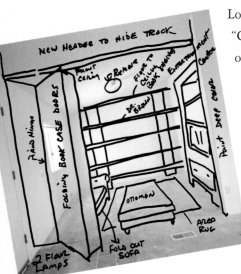

OPPOSITE: A small 10-by-10-foot area at the end of a long living room, just beyond the front door, was actually space provided to include some sort of den area.

THE SEVEN LAYERS

LAYER 1: PAINT AND ARCHITECTURE
Since this "room" was part of our Modern living room (see page 20), we used the same elements to unite both spaces. SpaceXDoors were hung and shelves were built from floor to ceiling. The paint colors were the reverse of the living room, with trim and ceiling remaining the same for continuity. Don't be afraid of rich wall color. It's the background to show off the things you love.

LAYER 2: INSTALLED FLOORING
The neutral living room wall-to-wall carpet continued into this room. Smart-looking area rugs can always be added. This works especially well for renters.

LAYER 3: HIGH-TICKET UPHOLSTERY
A sleeper sofa and ottomans provide flexible seating in tight quarters. When the sofa goes into bed mode, the ottomans wheel out into the living room. (Check out my home collection for cool ottomans with lift-up storage—even better!)

LAYER 4: ACCENT FABRICS
As in the living room, we stayed rich in background color but fairly monochromatic with accent fabrics. I love simple Roman shades in small spaces to keep this kind of room tailored. They are great with miniblinds, too.

LAYER 5: NONUPHOLSTERED SURFACES
Put a tray on the ottomans and they serve as coffee tables. We added the entertainment center. Note that its full scale in a small room actually makes the room look larger.

LAYER 6: ACCESSORIES
With our new shelves, you can go crazy with merchandising. But remember to consider the entire wall as you do your display, not just the shelf you are working on. Step back and make sure to disperse objects, colors, and themes evenly on the entire wall.

LAYER 7: PLANTS AND LIGHTING
A floor lamp works well if there's no room for a side table. Make sure switches are visible for your overnight guest. If tall plants take up too much room, a lovely floral plant on an ottoman tray can really do a lot of visual work.

SPACEXDOORS
HIDE-A-DOOR BOOKSHELF

To be comfortable, a guest needs at a minimum: a comfortable bed, a reading lamp, TV, and, most important of all, privacy. What? In the living room, just feet from the front door? Are you kidding? Well, read on.

"First things first" in this instance meant creating some kind of movable wall unit that would not only provide total privacy at night for the now-and-then guest but also return the area to the family space it was designed to be after the guest had gone. Well, we all scratched our heads until I remembered that we had had an in-studio guest on the show who built sliding bookshelf units that we thought were quite unusual and very cool. After some research we found the company: SpaceXDoors, a business that had developed a hinged bookcase for this very purpose.

Since the space had a vaulted ceiling, we had to create a header, or false beam, on which to attach a track. A similar track was attached to the floor directly below the first. This would be the device in which these amazing floor-to-ceiling bookcase "walls" could open and close. Once installed, two hinged SpaceXDoors would span the 10-foot opening. This would provide the flexibility we were looking for. When closed, the back of the bookcases would form a solid wall facing the existing living room; when open, a complete internal library would be revealed. After installation, we realized that we needed only one side of the bookcases to open. That was a boon, because the closed side then formed a permanent stationary foyer area at the front door, creating an anchor for the mirror we put there. (See page 40 for more details.) By the way, these shelves look almost seamless when they are closed, so show your guests how this system works before they bed down for the night—or they are not going to be able to find their way out in the morning.

Recessed on one side of the room, opposite a small window, we placed a full-size, warm wood entertainment center. We added a smallish TV to make room for guest wardrobe, towels, and the like. And under the window on the opposite wall we placed a convertible sofa that turned into a surprisingly

"Double duty doubles space. Ask yourself, 'What else can this thing do?'"

comfortable bed at night. Not all of these convertibles are created equal. If you want to keep your friends, we suggest that you take some time to try out such sofas at the store before you bring one home. This is also one of those rare instances when I'm going to tell you that it's okay to push the furniture right up against the wall. We simply don't have enough room to do anything else. And you know what? The room ended up looking fabulous anyway.

For storage we used every inch of vertical space, building in wall-to-wall book-cases from a series of boxes and shelves. (See page 155 for building instructions.) Simple plywood squares supported the first wooden shelf, then the next series of boxes supported the next shelf, and so on, starting from the floor and rising up to the ceiling. It's your basic cinder-block dorm furniture made more sophisticated with dynamic use of contrasting paint colors. A deep chocolate (Bitter Cocoa) was used to simulate wood stain on the shelves with a green sage (Roasted Celery) color in the background, and, of course, Lowell Lavender.

For the final accents, the lines of the shelves were continued around the adjacent walls, and a Roman shade elongated the small window, making it seem twice its actual size. Two ottomans were pushed together as a coffee table unit in front of the sofa. By day, when you sit in the tailored but comfortable sofa and put your feet up, you can relax and enjoy a movie or maybe a certain TV show (hint!). At night, the ottomans move outside of the room to create a cross-linking device between the library and the living room, and you have room to open the sofa into a double bed. You now have a small but open, totally dual-function space.

OPPOSITE: Behind the mirror are the movable folding SpaceX bookcases (see Resources). After installation, we realized that we needed only one side of the bookcases to open. That was great, because the closed side then formed a permanent stationary foyer area at the front door.

half-column and shelving

1 Draw a diagram of the shelving configuration using accurate measurements within the dimensions of the wall space. Take into account the location of light switches, wall receptacles, and heating vents.

3 Cut wood veneer for the edges of the shelves, glue to the edges, and attach with finishing nails. If the shelves will not extend wall to wall, finish the ends with veneer as well.

2 Each shelf is constructed of 3 thicknesses of ¾-inch MDF or plywood. Apply wood glue to the surfaces of the shelving boards, stack 3 of them together, and clamp in place. Screw the shelves together along the ends. Let dry.

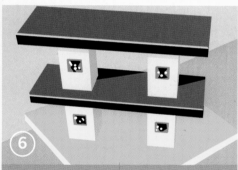

6 Assemble the shelving system by stacking shelves on top of columns and lining up the columns vertically. Attach wood squares to the top and underside of each shelf and slide the columns over the wood blocks.

4 Determine the number of upright columns needed for the shelving system and build four-sided boxes of the desired height and width. Glue and screw the 4 sides together. Construct all columns the same size.

5 Measure the inner dimensions of the opening of the column and cut squares of ¾-inch MDF or plywood for the top and bottom of each column. These wood blocks will secure the columns to the shelves, locking them into place.

7 Fill in screw holes with wood putty. Sand, prime with a stain-blocking primer, and paint.

Steps shown in miniature.

sun-sational room with a viewpoint

ONE OF THE MORE CHALLENGING spaces we had to deal with in the Small Spaces project was a tiny back room that connected the kitchen with a master bedroom. The inspiration here was my desire for a place where the entire family could kick back and feel like they were outdoors.

At one end it had a fairly large window opposite two doors on the other, so the potential for high traffic flow was  serious. We wanted to give the space an indoor-outdoor feeling with lots of organic elements, or at least the illusion of various natural textures. Here again, the small space was so furniture-unfriendly that there was barely enough room to put two pieces of anything, let alone a sofa. So we decided to practice what we preach.

We started with the concept of building wall to wall. It's a solution we used frequently with great success in other small areas of these houses. Out came the drawing pad as we devised a way to get multiple seating, hard surfaces, plus storage.

Looking for extra space? Look up, my dear. Overhead spaces can create focal points without taking up footprint. The overhead space was an easy call. Well above average human height, simple wooden cubbies were attached just above the window casements. We envisioned that these would be merchandised with lots of books, plants, and other objects that would read well when seen from below.

THE SEVEN LAYERS

LAYER 1: PAINT AND ARCHITECTURE
Faux was the word in this room. Remember, to prevent garish results when you are faux-finishing backgrounds, minimize the contrast between colors. The overhead cubbies can be made off-site, painted, then attached to the already painted walls.

LAYER 2: INSTALLED FLOORING
This space was off the kitchen, so it came with the same vinyl flooring. But a great area rug, added later, made the flooring disappear. We could also have painted the vinyl a rich terra-cotta finished with high-gloss polyurethane for a really dramatic look. In fact, now that I think about it . . . Oh, well!

LAYER 3: HIGH-TICKET UPHOLSTERY
Since all our cushions were part of our built-ins, we had the bucks to have them professionally done. Take your measurements to a foam retailer and let them use their cool electric saw while you wait. Again, the ottoman comes to the rescue. Put your feet up, or place trays on it for drinks and munchies.

LAYER 4: ACCENT FABRICS
Note how the eye goes right to those throw pillows. Change them to iridescent silk, and the room instantly goes formal. Add a bright yellow one and it's spring! Never underestimate the power of the pillow. The drapes were kept simple and tied in with the cushions.

LAYER 5: NONUPHOLSTERED SURFACES
With space at a premium, the tables were built right into the whole seating unit. Remember that a little Flex-all compound over a flea market find can transform almost any surface into stone.

LAYER 6: ACCESSORIES
Overscale organic pieces help ground this space with lots more terra-cotta and pottery. But make sure you leave room for your guests to effectively use those surfaces.

LAYER 7: PLANTS AND LIGHTING
Lamps with organic-toned bases and a rustic candle chandelier added mood, shadows, and intimacy. Tiny uplights exaggerated the foliage both at eye level and overhead.

As our greenhouse-library vision began to crystallize, the seating arrangement moved to the top of our agenda. We created a system of, you guessed it, more boxes and platforms, which, when all connected, would create "a modular U-shaped table and chair built-in doohickey." It seems I'm forever showing you how to build boxes, and we have shown zillions (okay, billions) of different ways, so I know everyone can do it. That's what makes what we do so simple. All these boxes can be made separately, then carried into the space. That's the best part— you're not stuck trying to lug some huge, heavy thing into the room all at once.

The structures we came up with for opposite walls were the same, adding symmetry and balance to the room. We placed one five-sided box in the corner, placed another five-sided box next to it with a cushion on top, then added a pedestal made from two stacked boxes, followed by another box with a cushion. The boxes that were destined to hold cushions were built shorter so that the

OPPOSITE: The wall-to-wall idea helps to effectively maximize every inch of space without intruding on the footprint of the room. The height of the pedestals was determined by what would be comfortable at elbow's length when seated. ABOVE: The overhead space was an easy call. Well above average human height, simple wooden cubbies were attached just above the window casements. We envisioned that these would be merchandised with lots of books and plants.

cushions would stay flush with the level of the corner boxes. As we came around to the adjacent wall, we had a nice big hard surface in the corner and another big box with a big cushion. That's all there is to it, just nine basic boxes. The wall-to-wall idea helps to effectively maximize every inch of space without intruding on the footprint of the room. The height of the pedestals was determined by what would be comfortable at elbow's length when seated.

Texture was crucial in this room to give it that indoor-outdoor feel, so we skim-coated Flex-all over all the exposed wood surfaces and tinted it a color called Pumpkin Pie to produce the stone look we were after. We loved the effect so much that we decided to simulate a Venetian plaster finish called Texston for the walls. (See instructions opposite.) The material was trawled on unevenly and left to dry. It was then sanded to a smooth, marblelike sheen. It added a charming, rich, old-world appearance.

Certain things should be left to a professional, and cutting foam is one of them. To be sure the cushions are cut very precisely, make a paper template and take it to the vendor that sells upholstery foam. They have got the proper equipment to cut it to the exact dimensions you need. That way the cushions look professionally done and have a custom fit.

We upholstered all of the cushions in a neutral stripe accent fabric that was also used to make the drapes. We wanted to keep the two identical, tying them together in such a small room. Other accent fabrics have been introduced in the

ABOVE: Confine specific patterns to things like pillows that can be easily replaced if you change your mind.

texston treatment

1 Mix sand with primer and apply to the wall to tooth the surface so that the Texston Marmorino plaster material will adhere. Let dry.

Load a clean trowel with the base color and 2 other colors of Texston, and mix lightly together. Apply the Texston in patches, leaving a small percentage of the first coat open. Blend the patches together with the trowel, leaving ridges for a distressed look. Work in 3-by-3-foot sections. Let dry.

3 Using a steel trowel, apply the Texston in the base color to the wall surface. The layer should be ⅛ inch thick. Hold the trowel at a 5-degree angle from the surface. Spread as evenly as possible. After the Texston is 80 to 90 percent dry, knock down any final ridges with the trowel. You can spray on water to make the surface slicker and easier to smooth. Let dry.

2 For each color you plan to use, mix a tint with the Texston Marmorino, or purchase a product already tinted. A mixing rod attached to a power drill can be used for mixing or mix by hand with a paint stick. Mix approximately 10 ounces of colorant per gallon of Texston. The product will dry approximately 40 to 50 percent lighter than it appears when wet.

5 The surface can be waxed with a solvent-based wax using a cotton cloth or electric polisher in a circular motion. Iridescent powder can also be added to the wax. Or a solvent or water-based penetrating sealer can be applied to the surface with a roller or garden sprayer instead of wax.

Complete instructions for the application of this and other Texston products are available through classes offered by Texston:

Texston
8239 Remmet Avenue
Canoga Park, CA 91304
Phone: 818-227-4812
Website: www.texston.com

> "When in doubt, go organic! Remember, there are no mistakes in nature."

form of solid, colorful dupioni silk pillows, which are scattered throughout the room. Remember that the eye is drawn to color, so use it with discretion. The pillows that look reminiscent of the Southwest were actually made from kilim and other kinds of Oriental rugs. And while we are on the subject of carpeting, let's not overlook the Indian area rug that effectively hides the drab wall-to-wall carpet we inherited.

So let's review. We now had seating for up to six and the center of the room was still empty, but not for long. In the middle of the room we placed an oversize ottoman for seating, use as a coffee table, or a place to put your feet up. The top opens, revealing plenty of storage for books, throws, and clutter that often make a small room look a tad messy. But we wanted even more storage. With the overhead shelves in place, banana baskets were then added to the cubbies. Since they're really portable, they're easy to take down, pull out what you need, and put back up. Ever mindful of our need to maximize space wherever possible, we even shoehorned storage under the pedestals as well. Bye-bye, clutter!

Something else in the retreat room that gave it that indoor-outdoor look: luxurious plants. They are set on overhead ledges, on the corner surfaces, and on the floor. Large palms are reflected in a mirror placed up against the wall, making the room look larger than it really is.

The lighting plan is simple, yet effective. We placed lamps with organic-toned bases on our higher boxes. Uplights behind the palms in the corners cast fabulous shadows on the ceiling. And in the center of the room we hung a wrought-iron chandelier holding real candles that looks as if we'd stumbled over it in an old Spanish hacienda.

When it comes to your small spaces, remember the wall-to-wall built-in concept. And don't forget those overhead spaces, too. Every inch counts, so make them work for you. And if you're thinking indoor-outdoor retreat, pull in plenty of organic texture and deep color and you, too, can start living alfresco. Al who? Oh, never mind. Just sit back, put your feet on the ottoman, and brush up on your Italian.

A CLOSE LOOK BACK at the "before" shots of the rooms in these two empty houses, with their all-white walls and vacant floors, will reveal much smaller, more cramped-feeling spaces than their "after" counterparts now that they have been filled with glorious color, texture, and volume. If we could do it in this small space, you can do it in yours!

OPPOSITE: Ever mindful of our need to maximize space wherever possible, we even shoehorned storage under the pedestals as well.

Don't Cut Corners

KEEPING corners from becoming visual cul-de-sacs can be diffi-
cult but is certainly not impossible. Many throw up their hands in
despair when faced with a nook or a cranny, while others try to
deny its existence. A good corner doesn't necessarily cry out for a
lot of stuff, but the right objects can make all the difference. Most
corners lie outside the usual high-traffic areas, which makes them
suitable for large objects we might trip over elsewhere, such as
palms or topiary. Storage in the form of shelving can work really
well in a corner as long as you leave access to it. The shelves
become an integral part of the room's overall design and leave
plenty of space to play with collections and accessories. Do you fill
them up with nothing but books, or are tchotchkes more your
style? Perhaps it's a combination of the two, punctuated by the
occasional plant.

Wall art can live exceptionally well in a corner as does a mirror
of nearly any shape. A painting that is well proportioned to the wall space available over
a console supporting a vase can be
a knockout. Ignore your corners at your peril. You could
wind up with a room where
all the furniture looks like it
has been shoved into the
center. Filling the corners
grounds the space and keeps
it from floating.

**LEFT: Something else in the
retreat room gave it that
indoor-outdoor look: fabulous
plants. They are set on
overhead ledges, on the corner
surfaces, and on the floor.
Large palms are reflected in a
mirror placed up against the wall, making the
room look larger than it really is. An old-world wrought-iron
chandelier creates a focal point in the center of the room.**

the seven layers of design

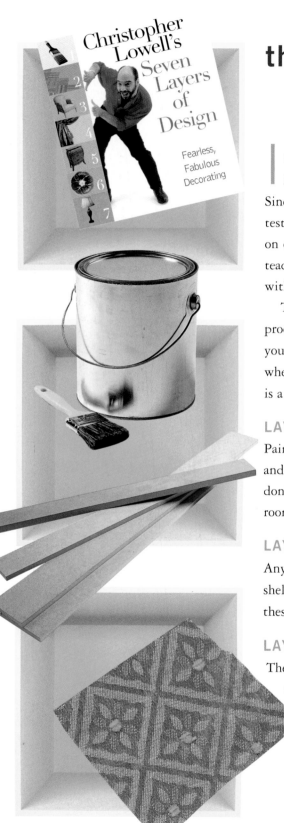

I N MY FIRST BOOK, *Christopher Lowell's Seven Layers of Design: Fearless, Fabulous Decorating,* we take an in-depth look at the Seven Layers of Design. Since its first publishing, it has been reprinted some thirteen times. Rigorously tested by more than three thousand men and women prior to its debut in 1995 on our first series, *Interior Motives,* it has been at the epicenter of everything we teach. Since then thousands of American viewers have implemented the system with great success.

The Seven Layers are a sequential road map that breaks down the design process a layer at a time to not only help you get the project done but also keep you on budget. Most important, the design process is divided into seven areas where you might get bogged down and overwhelmed. For your convenience, here is a brief overview of that process.

LAYER 1: PAINT AND ARCHITECTURE

Paint is one of the most effective and inexpensive ways to add substance, warmth, and "theme" to any room. But remember this golden rule: If you paint the walls, don't forget to paint the ceiling, too. A touch of molding will give charmless rooms substance and add value to your property.

LAYER 2: INSTALLED FLOORING

Anything that runs from wall to wall, such as wood, tile, or carpet, completes the shell of the room. Choose something neutral in color. Furniture will interrupt these expanses, so be sure to consider how much of the floor you are going to see.

LAYER 3: HIGH-TICKET UPHOLSTERY

The fabric on sofas, club chairs, and settees should be textural and solid rather than busy motifs that might be costly to change later when you tire of them. To avoid this pattern trap, reserve your prints for Layer 4, and keep these background fabrics versatile.

LAYER 4: ACCENT FABRICS

Accent fabrics are those drapes, pillows, runners, and table toppers that help bring a room alive. Because they are more affordable to replace, they can be changed seasonally or when the pattern becomes dated. Area rugs are also part of this layer and are ideal centerpieces for conversation groupings.

LAYER 5: NONUPHOLSTERED SURFACES

We call these the workhorses of the room. Tables, desks, bookcases, and armoires all help make a room functional, as well as provide storage. If your seating is clustered in a conversation grouping in the center of your room, then the walls can be left free for these necessary pieces. It is a good idea to keep surfaces at arm's length of those seated for convenience. Remember: The human form needs only 18 to 20 inches between items to comfortably navigate in a room, so when choosing a coffee table, big is better!

LAYER 6: ACCESSORIES

This layer includes wall art, vases, artwork, mirrors, and just about any decorative tabletop piece. Think in terms of fewer large-scale items rather than an abundance of small ones, which can easily get absorbed into a room and create "room dandruff."

LAYER 7: PLANTS AND LIGHTING

These two elements are combined to create shadows, lending an air of intimacy to a room. As much light should be coming from the floor as from the ceiling; an uplight under a large-scale tree casts dramatic ceiling shadows, while task lamps add function and decoration to a space. The flicker of candlelight adds a warmly romantic and cozy feeling. Recess, spot, or track lighting helps draw the eye to specific objects of interest. Washed light on richly colored walls accentuates surface texture and artwork.

For a more detailed explanation of these layers and how to use them, please refer to *Christopher Lowell's Seven Layers of Design: Fearless, Fabulous Decorating,* available in bookstores or online at www.christopherlowell.com.

resources

MODERN LIVING ROOM

Paint: Christopher Lowell Designer Paint (walls: Mocha Mauve, Portabella; ceiling: Walnut Shell; trim: Bitter Cocoa)

Shelves: IKEA

Rugs: Media Meridian

Furniture, curtains, fabrics: Broyhill Furniture

Accessories: Brett Austin Group; Burlington Coat Factory; Douglas Hill Photography; IKEA

Lighting: Casual Lamps

Plants: Trees International

TRADITIONAL LIVING ROOM

Paint: Christopher Lowell Designer Paint (walls: Braised Cantaloupe, Pumpkin Pie; ceiling: Roasted Celery; trim: Buttermilk)

Molding: Balmer Studios

Rugs: Oriental Weavers of America

Furniture, curtains, fabrics: Flexsteel Industries

Accessories: Burlington Coat Factory

Table lamps: Sedgefield by Adam

Plants: Trees International

MODERN FOYER

Paint: Christopher Lowell Designer Paint (walls: Portabella; ceiling: Walnut Shell; trim: Bitter Cocoa)

Swinging doors: SpaceXDoors

Demitable: Brett Austin Group

Rug: Brett Austin Group

Photography: Douglas Hill Photography

Mirror: Stanley Furniture

Lighting: Casual Lamps

Plants: Trees International

TRADITIONAL ENTRYWAY

Paint: Christopher Lowell Designer Paint (walls: Braised Cantaloupe, Pumpkin Pie; ceiling: Roasted Celery; trim: Buttermilk)

Molding: Balmer Studios

Mirror: Stanley Furniture

Accessories: Burlington Coat Furniture

Sofa table: Flexsteel Industries

MODERN MASTER BEDROOM

Paint: Christopher Lowell Designer Paint (walls: Pale Pesto; ceiling: Roasted Celery; lattice undercoat/top coat: Braised Cantaloupe/Pale Oregano; bed: Bitter Cocoa)

Bamboo products: Loose Ends

Rugs: Media Meridian

Dresser, lattice cubes, lighting: IKEA

Leather ottoman: Broyhill Furniture

Bedding, mirrors, curtains, fabrics: Burlington Coat Factory

Accessories: Brett Austin Group

Lighting: Casual Lamps

Plants: Trees International

MODERN MASTER BATH

Paint: Christopher Lowell Designer Paint (walls: Braised Cantaloupe; ceiling: Roasted Celery; trim: Green Tea)

Bamboo products: Loose Ends

Linens: Burlington Coat Factory

Lighting: IKEA

Area rug: Media Meridian

Accessories: Burlington Coat Factory, IKEA

Plants: Trees International

TRADITIONAL MASTER BEDROOM

Paint: Christopher Lowell Designer Paint (walls: Huckleberry Dust; ceiling color: Lilac Sorbet; trim: Crème Brûlée)

Molding: Balmer Studios

Rug: Oriental Weavers of America

Curtains, linens: Burlington Coat Factory

Lighting: IKEA

Plants: Trees International

TRADITIONAL MASTER BATH

Paint: Christopher Lowell Designer Paint (walls: Lilac
   Sorbet; ceiling: Huckleberry Dust; trim: White Crackle
   Finish)

Molding: Van Dyke Restorers

Furniture: Linens 'n Things

Curtains: Waverly Fabrics

Linens: Burlington Coat Factory

Accessories: Linens 'n Things; Burlington Coat Factory

Lighting: IKEA

Rug: Oriental Weavers of America

Plants: Trees International

MODERN GUESTROOM

Paint: Christopher Lowell Designer Paint (walls: Portabella;
   ceiling: Cookie Dough; trim: Bitter Cocoa; built-in:
   Walnut Shell)

Upholstered ottoman, fabric for curtains: Broyhill Furniture

Linens, Pillows: Burlington Coat Factory

Accessories: Linens 'n Things; Burlington Coat Factory

Rug: Media Meridian

Lighting: IKEA

Plants: Trees International

LOUIS XV GUEST BEDROOM

Paint: Christopher Lowell Designer Paint (walls: Smoked
   Trout; ceiling color: Clam Shell; trim: Blue Points)

Lincrusta: Van Dyke Restorers

Molding: Balmer Studios

Rug: Oriental Weavers of America

Furniture: Stanley Furniture

Linens (Christopher Lowell Collection), lighting: Burlington
   Coat Factory

Curtains: Waverly Fabrics

Accessories: Brett Austin Group

Plants: Trees International

BOMBAY SLEIGH BED

Paint: Christopher Lowell Designer Paint (walls: Apple Skin,
   Saffron; ceiling: Apple Juice; trim: Gold)

Molding, wainscotting (anaglypta): Van Dyke Restorers

Furniture: Stanley Furniture

Linens (Christopher Lowell Collection), accessories: Burlington
   Coat Factory

Curtains: Burlington Coat Factory, Waverly Fabrics

Rug: Oriental Weavers of America

Lighting: Sedgefield by Adam

Sconces: IKEA

Bamboo products: Loose Ends

Caning: Van Dyke Restorers

TRADITIONAL GUEST BATHROOM

Paint: Christopher Lowell Designer Paint (walls and ceiling:
   Burnt Plum; trim: White)

Linens: Burlington Coat Factory

Accessories: Linens 'n Things; IKEA

Plants: Trees International

MODERN GUEST BATHROOM

Paint: Christopher Lowell Designer Paint (walls: Melon
   Brine; ceiling: Crème de Menthe; trim: Green Tea)

Storage boxes, accessories: IKEA

Linens: Burlington Coat Factory

MODERN UTILITY ROOM AND WORKSTATION

Paint: Christopher Lowell Designer Paint (walls and ceiling:
   Nutmeg Rose; trim: Shitake)

Furniture: IKEA

Accessories: IKEA; Linens 'n Things

TRADITIONAL DINING ROOM

Paint: Christopher Lowell Designer Paint (walls: Walnut Shell; ceiling: Roasted Celery; trim: Buttermilk)

Molding: Balmer Studios

Rug: Oriental Weavers of America

Furniture: Stanley Furniture

Curtains: Waverly Fabrics

Lighting: Casual Lamps; IKEA

Plants: Trees International

MODERN KITCHEN/DINING AREA

Paint: Christopher Lowell Designer Paint (walls: Creamed Asparagus; ceiling: Walnut Shell; cabinets and work table: Crème Brûlée; trim: Shitake; recessed shelves: Hammerite Silver)

Wall materials: Loose Ends

Rugs: Media Meridian

Furniture (kitchen): IKEA

Furniture (dining area): Broyhill Furniture

Appliance refacing material: Frigo Design

Curtains: Broyhill Furniture

Accessories: IKEA; Brett Austin Group

Mirror: Stanley Furniture

Lighting: IKEA

Plants: Trees International

TRADITIONAL KITCHEN

Paint: Christopher Lowell Designer Paint (walls: Braised Cantaloupe, Pumpkin Pie; ceiling color: Roasted Celery; trim color: Buttermilk)

Molding: Balmer Studios

Corbels/table base: Van Dyke Restorers

Rug: Oriental Weavers of America

Chair: Stanley Furniture

Demitable: Brett Austin Group

Settee, curtains: Flexsteel

Appliance refacing material: Frigo

Accessories: Linens 'n Things

Lighting: IKEA

Plants: Trees International

MODERN FAMILY ROOM

Paint: Christopher Lowell Designer Paint (walls: Mocha Mauve, Portabella; ceiling: Walnut Shell; trim: Bitter Cocoa)

Swinging doors: SpaceXDoors

Rug: Media Meridian

Leather sofas, case goods, curtains: Broyhill Furniture

Bedding, pillows: Burlington Coat Factory

Accessories: Brett Austin Group; Burlington Coat

Lighting: Casual Lamps

Plants: Trees International

TRADITIONAL SUNROOM

Paint: Christopher Lowell Designer Paint (ceiling: Cookie Dough)

Venetian plaster walls: Texston

Rug: Oriental Weavers of America

Ottoman: Flexsteel Industries

Curtains/cushions: Waverly Fabrics

Pillows, accessories: IKEA

Lighting: Casual Lamps

Plants: Trees International

contact information

Balmer Studios: 203-227-1419; www.balmerstudios.com

Brett Austin Group: 410-358-6082

Broyhill Furniture: 828-758-3328; www.broyhillfurn.com

Burlington Coat Factory: 609-387-7800; www.coat.com

Casual Lamps: 213-321-0180

Christopher Lowell Designer Paint Collection: www.christopherlowell.com

Douglas Hill Photography: 323-660-0681; www.doughill.com

Flexsteel Industries: 800-685-SOFA; www.flexsteel.com

Frigo Design: 800-836-8746; www.frigodesign.com

IKEA: 800-434-IKEA; www.ikea.com

Linens 'n Things: 973-778-1300; www.lnt.com

Loose Ends: 503-390-2348; www.looseends.com

Media Meridian: 562-494-9266

Oriental Weavers of America: 800-858-5749; www.owarug.com

SpaceXDoors: 800-262-9464; www.spacexdoors.com

Stanley Furniture: 276-627-2000; www.stanleyfurniture.com

Texston: 800-788-7113; www.texston.com

Trees International: 888-873-3799; www.treesinternational.com

Van Dyke Restorers: 800-787-3355; www.vandykes.com

Waverly Fabrics: 212-213-7899; www.decoratewaverly.com

acknowledgments

Y OU'VE HEARD ME SAY IT A MILLION TIMES: "Nothing happens by
yourself." So, as always, I want to thank my loyal viewers of *The Christopher
Lowell Show.*. Your ideas, questions, and suggestions are truly my inspiration.
This book also took the efforts of many special people. To my editorial staff of
Doug Hill, Kevin Newman, Frances Schultz, and Elayne Sawaya, thank you for
your dedication. I thank Janet Newell for detailing the projects, and Jocelyne
Borys and her talented crew, which includes Paul Meek, Steven Burright, and
Nathan Smith, for making these spaces look amazing. Thanks to Dana Neillie
for finding the small spaces. To everyone who worked in the sweltering heat on
the Fleetwood site, in Riverside, California, during July and August 2001—we
survived! Thanks to Sohayla Cude for her coordination. Michael Murphy for
filling in the gaps. Laura Ellegard for communicating my thoughts to you, the
viewers and fans. My team at *The Christopher Lowell Show.* All my friends
at the Discovery Channel, especially Judith McHale, Clark Bunting,
Jamie Grossman-Young, Susan Murrow, and Carol LeBlanc. Gerri
Leonard for keeping us on budget, I think, and to my business man-
agement team at Sendyk, Leonard & Co., thanks for your years
of support. Lauren Shakely and the incredible group at Clarkson
Potter, including Maggie Hinders, Max Werner, Mark McCauslin, and
Joan Denman. And Douglas Hill, again, thank you for the great
photos. And lastly, many thanks to my dear friend and partner
Daniel J. Levin, and the staff of Levin Entertainment Co.

index